Negotiated Sovereignty

Negotiated Sovereignty

*Working to Improve
Tribal-State Relations*

JEFFREY S. ASHLEY AND
SECODY J. HUBBARD

Westport, Connecticut
London

Library of Congress Cataloging-in-Publication Data

Ashley, Jeffrey S., 1965–
  Negotiated sovereignty : working to improve tribal-state relations / Jeffrey S. Ashley and Secody J. Hubbard.
    p. cm.
  Includes bibliographical references and index.
  ISBN 0–275–96949–5 (alk. paper)
    1. Indians of North America—Government relations. 2. Indians of North America—Politics and government. 3. Indians of North America—Legal status, laws, etc. 4. Tribal government—United States. 5. Federal government—United States. 6. State governments—United States—States. 7. Intergovernmental cooperation—United States. 8. Self-determination, National—United States. I. Hubbard, Secody J. II. Title.
E93.A85 2004
323.1′197073—dc21   2003046309

British Library Cataloguing in Publication Data is available.

Copyright © 2004 by Jeffrey S. Ashley and Secody J. Hubbard

All rights reserved. No portion of this book may be
reproduced, by any process or technique, without the
express written consent of the publisher.

Library of Congress Catalog Card Number: 2003046309
ISBN: 0–275–96949–5

First published in 2004

Praeger Publishers, 88 Post Road West, Westport, CT 06881
An imprint of Greenwood Publishing Group, Inc.
www.praeger.com

Printed in the United States of America

The paper used in this book complies with the
Permanent Paper Standard issued by the National
Information Standards Organization (Z39.48-1984).

10 9 8 7 6 5 4 3 2 1

Contents

I.	**The History and Background**	1
1	Introduction	3
2	The Setting: Federalism, Intergovernmental Relations, and Vacillating Views toward Tribal Governments	13
3	Sovereignty and the State-Tribal Relationship	27
II.	**Real World Tribal-State Interaction**	43
4	The Campo Band of Kumeyaay Indians	45
5	The Navajo Nation	57
6	The Puyallup Tribe	69
7	The Confederated Salish-Kootenai Tribes of the Flathead Nation	79
8	The Shoshone-Bannock Tribes	91
9	The St. Regis Mohawk Nation	103
III.	**Looking Forward**	117
10	Conclusion: New Directions for State-Tribal Relations	119
Bibliography		127
Index		133

PART I
The History and Background

CHAPTER 1

Introduction

> A new policy and institutional framework for state-tribal relations must be developed that is cognizant of previous policy and legal rulings as well as the current reality of Indian self-determination.
> —Council of State Governments

Most people in America today fail to recognize that intergovernmental relations encompasses interaction between not only the federal and state governments but also with Indian nations. The latter presents a much more perplexing status than the former within the American federal system of government. The status of American Indian tribes as sovereigns within the American political system is perplexing, since they are neither completely absorbed in the traditional scheme of federalism nor are they completely separated from the American political system. This has led some to argue that Indian nations are outside the U.S. political system,[1] creating a third domestic sovereign recognized by the constitution.[2] Others, however erroneously, have argued that tribes are not really sovereign at all and are nothing more than another racial minority residing within our nation's borders.[3] Needless to say, the role of tribal governments in the American political system is complex, generally misunderstood, and often ignored.

Because of federal Indian policy that has shifted between assimilation and Indian self-determination, the exact status of these unique enclaves has remained uncertain. Hence the relationship is sometimes referred to as the "Indian problem." The tribes have been seen as obstacles to the larger polity in natural resource acquisition and other matters. This has led to conflict. To complicate the current relations, a complex array of federal legislation and judicial decisions that seem to lack consistency and coherence have resulted in no clear statutory guidelines for either state or tribal governments to follow. Rather, through case law, treaties, and federal and state statutes, federal Indian reserves find themselves in a confusing and bizarre jurisdictional framework of intergovernmental relations. This arrangement "creates bewildering challenges to tribal and state officials charged with administering justice and performing governmental responsibility."[4]

Much has been written about the intergovernmental relations between the federal government and the states. Among the works on the state-federal relationship are the many American government textbooks that discuss federalism and the shared power between states and the national government. Through these texts, the majority of American citizens and policy makers understand the role of states and the federal government. Indian nations, however, are less often studied and are therefore often misplaced when people examine the complex relationship between states, the federal government, and tribal governments.[5] Much like texts, which are often viewed as sources of authority, other sources of information tend to ignore tribal governments in the federal system.[6] This is particularly true of state-tribal relations. For example, Frank Pommersheim notes that a law review literature search for a four-year period revealed that of more than 300 Indian law articles, notes, and comments, less than three percent focus on issues of tribal-state relations.[7] Likewise, David Wilkins says that "while tribal and state relations invoke and entail a host of substantive political (intergovernmental), constitutional and extra-constitutional, social, legal, and extra-legal, and cross-cultural issues and concerns, there remains a paucity of scholarly literature on the dynamics of this interracial, intercultural, and interjurisdictional area."[8] Wilkins notes that it is understandable, yet unfortunate, that the overwhelming majority of the literature deals with the federal-tribal relationship to the exclusion of any exploration of the complex nature of state-tribal interaction. If relations are to ever improve, people need to be able to read about the unique position that tribes hold in America.

Federal Indian reserves are misunderstood nations within a nation. As such, intergovernmental relations are often characterized by mistrust, anger, frustration, and fear. Inadequate treatment in the literature aside, this misunderstanding can be attributed largely to the historical legal interpretation of the relationship between the federal government and Indian tribes. As a noted legal scholar on Indian law and policy, Vine Deloria, has written, "federal Indian law itself is a mythical creature because it is composed of badly written, vaguely phrased and ill considered federal statutes: hundreds of self-serving solicitor's opinions and regulations; and state, federal, and Supreme Court decisions which bear little relationship to rational thought and contain a fictional view of American history."[9] In addition to being subject to confusing laws, these unique enclaves embody political, social, and economic conditions that are uncharacteristic of the larger society. These conditions have fostered the formulation and implementation of differing forms of policy in an ongoing effort to deal with the "Indian problem." The Indian problem throughout the development of federal-Indian relations and policy has traditionally encompassed the idea that Native Americans were legal and political obstacles to European expansion from east to west. The focus has specifically been on how to gain access to Indian resources, establish control over Indians, and subsequently transform native peoples into non-Indians. This, naturally, has led to Indian resistance.[10]

For most of the nineteenth century, federal-tribal government relations were formulated without the participation of indigenous peoples. Rather, policies were theoretically constituted conjectures that were not only predicated on the assumptions of Euro-American ideology and implemented in an asymmetrical hierarchical fashion, but also devised by policy makers who only had a distant identification with Indian reserves. As Cornell and Kalt observed, "For over a century . . . Indian tribes not only have been denied control of their own resources but have been largely excluded from the effective participation in major decisions affecting their own futures. Yet those who have held effective decision-making power, such as the BIA, have perverse incentives and/or have seldom had to bear the consequences of their decisions."[11] The effects have been a century of policy failures, confusion, expropriation of land, and severe economic disparity.[12] This, too, has had a detrimental impact on any move toward cooperation and trust between tribal governments and other sovereigns.

CHANGING RULES: SELF-DETERMINATION AND NEW FEDERALISM

Beginning in the 1960s, two separate, yet related, policies started pushing states and tribes closer together and in increasing conflict—the push for Indian self-determination and the move toward decentralization of federal programs.

Self-Determination

Since the 1960s and 1970s, Indian reserves have made tremendous progress both legally and politically. Since the 1970s, mostly through the policy of self-determination promulgated in 1975 under the Nixon administration, the ideas of self-sufficiency and self-governance have reigned. The philosophy of Indian self-rule gave tribes greater control of their own futures and reservation governments. This has meant substantial changes in government relations. While the policy of Indian self-rule brought a sense of renewal and resurgence to American Indian policy administration, control over reservation resources has increasingly brought tribes into conflict with state and local governments over jurisdictional issues and property rights.[13] Subsequently, relations between Indian nations and federal, state, and local governments have been marked by intergovernmental jurisdictional conflict over tribal peoples, natural resources, and property rights.

From 1980 through the mid-1990s, several major environmental laws were amended to preclude states from regulating environmental matters on Indian reserves. These included the Safe Drinking Water Act, the Super Fund Law, and the 1990 Clean Air Act (CAA). State governments were directed to treat Indian tribes as states for purposes of participating in the regulation, management, and implementation of environmental programs on reservations.[14] While these provisions have been critical in getting some states and tribes to look toward cooperative agreements and joint management, such forced cooperation has not been universally embraced. In many cases, forcing the hands of the state has not helped already strained relations between states and tribal governments.

New Federalism

In 1972 President Nixon sought to decentralize the administration of fiscal sources and grants. Nixon's New Federalism was advocated in response to fears that the national government had grown too large and intrusive. It was felt that state and local governments should be given more discretion to deal with state-local needs.[15] Likewise, the Reagan administration's New Federalism emphasized the separation of national and state functions. The administration favored a decentralization of power and policy control to states and local governments, such as giving responsibilities for social programs to the states (e.g., Medicaid, Food Stamps, Aid For Dependent Children (AFDC)). Although all of Reagan's specific proposals were not adopted, the basic idea was that there would be a swap in responsibilities with the states and a return of power to the states.[16]

President George Bush extended Reagan's agenda, and President Bill Clinton continued to push state and local governments to innovate. Clinton went even further by encouraging the establishment of partnerships among the federal, state, local, and tribal governments under the Reinventing Government movement.[17] Under the Clinton framework, tribes were viewed as sovereigns and were treated like states with regard to the administration of federal regulations.

On April 29, 1994, Clinton and his cabinet met with 300 Native American leaders to express his commitment to "consult with and work with tribal governments within the framework of a government-to-government relationship."[18] For the first time in the nation's history, a president of the United States and all members of his cabinet had met with representatives of Indian nations. With the trend toward decentralization, Indian tribes have been given responsibility for the development and implementation of many policies that impact them.

While President Clinton was the first president to have such a large-scale meeting, various administrations have attempted to consider tribes in the development of policy. For example, some of the power of the Bureau of Indian Affairs (BIA) was devolved directly to tribes as a part of President Johnson's War on Poverty.[19] The trend toward working with Indian tribal governments, fostering relationships, and including them in environmental legislation began with the Carter administration's creation of an Indian Work Group in 1980. The work of this group was instrumental in the 1984 adoption by the Environmental Protection Agency (EPA) of a policy that recognized tribal authority to develop tribal environmental programs. This policy established several guiding principles for governments to follow when working with Indian tribes. These principles included:

- Working with tribes on a government-to-government basis;
- Recognizing tribal authority to set standards, make decisions, and manage reservation programs;
- Encouraging cooperation between tribal and state governments;
- Removing legal and procedural impediments to working directly with tribes.[20]

Unfortunately, while self-determination and self-governance of Indian tribes has been the general policy of the federal government for a number of years, creating a partnership to achieve these objectives has not been easy. While President Clinton mandated a "tribes as states" approach at the federal level, and the EPA has been at the forefront of emphasizing tribal-federal cooperation, the agency that handles most tribal relations, and is entrusted to act as trustee on behalf of the U.S. government on matters related to tribal property, is the Bureau of Indian Affairs.

The BIA has never been fully trusted by tribes, and has recently been the target of numerous lawsuits stemming from the agency's management problems and misappropriation of tribal funds. For example, in 1996 an audit of the BIA revealed that the agency had made undocumented transactions in the amount of 2.4 billion dollars over a period of 20 years. These funds involved mineral royalties and other income held in trust by the BIA under the auspices of the Interior Department.[21] Mistrust of the BIA leaves many tribes feeling that any cooperation is a bad idea. To many, cooperating with the BIA has never been and will never be in the best interest of the tribe, because the BIA is not treating the tribal governments as independent nations. Despite some improvement, Indian scholar David Wilkins notes that the BIA record is uneven.[22] Perhaps the problem lies in institutional paternalism—the standards and operating procedures of the agency preclude it from ever really letting go and allowing the tribes to govern themselves. Organizations are like society in that they have cultures, and these cultures are sometimes slow to evolve. Perhaps this is why some of the newer agencies such as the EPA are able to actively pursue the self-government initiative and only provide necessary help, while the BIA is operating under the old rules.[23]

Just as all federal agencies have not fully adopted the tribes-as-states position, not all states have followed the lead of the U.S. government. While there have been some areas of state-tribal negotiation, cooperation, and shared management, overall success has proven to be elusive. Relations between state and tribal governments are often predicated not on shared governmental interests, but on differing perspectives on the issue of jurisdiction. Indeed the adversarial perceptions held by the federal, state, and tribal governments have been pervasive in Indian/non-Indian relations. Hence, state and tribal government relations have often been based on conflict rather than working within a framework of shared governmental interests. This is unfortunate, as many issues facing both states and tribes are of mutual concern. If there is to be any stability in the face of changing policy, technology, information, and public expectations of government responsiveness, "relations between the tribe and the federal and state governments must be stabilized, and mutual respect and parity in political rights must be established . . . A change in perception by both Indians and federal and state officials who deal with Indians is imperative if any substantial progress is to be achieved in the future."[24] Such a change in perception and respect will hinge upon a greater level of understanding.

A better understanding of the role that tribal governments play in the federal system is critical if we are to hope for greater cooperation between governments—something that is vitally important for several reasons. Understanding the conditions necessary for state-tribal cooperation is important because the decentralization of the American political system that began with Nixon's New Federalism in the early 1970s is very much an ingrained part of public policy as we begin the twenty-first century. The devolution under way is not likely to end, and power will undoubtedly continue to flow back to state, local, and tribal governments.

Another obvious reason for greater cooperation between state and tribal governments is that it involves a large number of people and a large amount of land. Numerous states have Indian tribes within their boundaries, and conflicts between those tribes and state governments appear to be increasing. It is imperative, therefore, that we understand what those relations are and how they can be improved so that common problems can be solved. These common problems include such things as crime, pollution, child welfare, and preservation of natural resources, which tend to have a spillover effect. As public goods, resources such as air and water are shared by all in a geographical area and know no jurisdictional boundaries. Thus, the problem of nonappropriability and a sense of responsibility from one government to another in providing for clean air and water dictate cooperation among governmental jurisdictions. It is important, if not crucial, that we better understand the conditions under which several governments can cooperate to succeed in environmental management and other areas of mutual concern.

Chapters 2 and 3 provide the background behind both federal-tribal and state-tribal relations. Such a foundation is necessary before embarking on any examination of intergovernmental relations. The federal-state-tribal relationship as it has evolved over time has, to a great extent, predetermined any attempts at state-tribal cooperation. Against an uncertain federal-tribal backdrop, states and tribes have often engaged in practices that tend to make things even worse. Historic tension between the states and tribes is an issue that needs to be explored prior to any discussion about forging new relationships and embarking on the future.

After a look at the legal and historical background needed for further exploration, chapters 4–9 offer six individual cases of state-tribal cooperative efforts and delve into their successes and failures. The six cases, selected from diverse parts of the country because of a varying degree of positive relations, provide us with both the positive and negative in terms of state-tribal cooperation. By doing this, we are able to isolate those variables that appear to be critical in forging new relationships, identify the conditions that help or work against fostering intergovernmental cooperation, and develop a more effective strategy for approaching policy from a cooperative standpoint.

Establishing partnerships that address mutual concerns is a benefit to the citizenry of both the reservation and the state. It is a fundamental responsibility of all governments to achieve a working relationship, since both the tribes and states affect each other so powerfully. In the future, states and tribes will need to focus even more on those aspects found in positive relationships, while ridding themselves of the negative tendencies that have plagued states and tribes over time. Clarifying these positive and negative conditions and offering suggestions for implementing a new framework for state-tribal cooperation are the focus of the book's conclusion and are offered as a handbook for state, tribal, and federal decision makers; students; and concerned citizens who see cooperation as the path toward a better society.

NOTES

1. Rudolph C. Ryser, "When Tribes and States Collide: A Special Report Prepared for the Inter-Tribal Study Group on Tribal/State Relations 1995," http://www.cwis.org/FWDP/Americas/collide1.htm (2 October 1996).
2. Charles F. Wilkinson and Eric R. Biggs, "The Evolution of the Termination Policy," *American Indian Law Review* 5 (1977), pp. 152–54.
3. Mark Anthony Rolo, "Indians Will Resist Gorton's Attempts to Rewrite Laws," *Seattle Times*, 4 September 1997.
4. David H. Getches, "Negotiated Sovereignty: Intergovernmental Agreements with American Indian Tribes as Models for Expanding Self-Government," *Review of Constitutional Studies*, vol. 1, no. 1 (1993), p. 121.
5. Jeffrey S. Ashley and Karen Jarratt-Ziemski, "Superficiality and Bias: The (Mis)Treatment of Native Americans in American Government Textbooks," *American Indian Quarterly*, vol. 23, nos. 3&4 (fall 1999), p. 49.
6. Ibid.
7. Frank Pommersheim, "Tribal State Relations: Hope for the Future?" *South Dakota Law Review* 36 (1991), p. 239.
8. David E. Wilkins, "Reconsidering the Tribal-State Compact Process," *Policy Studies Journal*, vol. 22, no. 3 (1994), p. 475.
9. Vine Deloria, Jr., "Laws Founded on Justice and Humanity: Reflections on the Content and Character of Federal Indian Law," *Arizona Law Review*, vol. 31 (fall 1989), p. 202.
10. Stephen Cornell, *The Return of the Native: American Indian Political Resurgence* (New York: Oxford University Press, 1988).
11. Stephen Cornell and Joseph P. Kalt, "Public Choice, Culture, and American Indian Economic Development" (Harvard University, 1988), http://www.KSG.Harvard.edu/hpaied/docs/PRS88-13.pdf.
12. Sharon O'Brien, *American Indian Tribal Governments* (Norman, OK: University of Oklahoma Press, 1989).
13. Cornell and Kalt, 1988, pp. 10–12, 21.
14. James B. Reed and Judy A. Zelio, *States and Tribes: Building New Traditions* (Washington, D.C.: National Conference of State Legislatures, 1995).
15. David Nice and Patricia Frederickson, *The Politics of Intergovernmental Relations* (Chicago: Nelson-Hall Publishers, 1995), p. 3.
16. Christopher Hamilton and Donald T. Wells, *Federalism, Power, and Political Economy* (Englewood Cliffs, NJ: Prentice Hall, 1990).
17. William A. Galston and Geoffrey L. Tibbetts, "Reinventing Federalism: The Clinton/Gore Program for a New Partnership among the Federal, State, Local, and Tribal Governments," *Publius: The Journal of Federalism* 24 (summer 1994), p. 23.
18. Office of the White House, "Government to Government Relations with Native American Tribal Governments," 29 April 1994.
19. O'Brien, pp. 86–91, 261–75.
20. U.S. Environmental Protection Agency, *EPA Policy for the Administration of Environmental Programs on Indian Reservations*, 8 November 1984.
21. Bill Donovan, "Big Money Is Topic of Phoenix," *Navajo Times*, 9 January 1997, p. A-2.
22. David Wilkins, *American Indian Politics and the American Political System* (New York: Rowman and Littlefield, 2002), p. 90.

23. LaDonna Harris, Stephen Sachs, and Barbara Morris, "Honoring the Circle: Developing Government-to-Government Relations between Tribal Governments and the Federal, State, and Local Governments" (paper presented at annual meeting of the Western Social Science Association, Albuquerque, NM, 2002).

24. Vine Deloria, Jr., and Clifford M. Lytle, *The Nations Within: The Past and Future of American Indian Sovereignty* (New York: Pantheon Books, 1984), pp. 234–64.

CHAPTER 2

The Setting: Federalism, Intergovernmental Relations, and Vacillating Views toward Tribal Governments

> The United States federal system consists of three primary parts—national, state and local (county and municipal) governments. The effective exercise of governmental authorities is made possible through a system of charters and constitutions which serve as the basis of the U.S. federation. There is a very important element missing from the United States federation—THE TRIBES . . . where do tribal governments fit into the federal and state system of government?[1]

Federalism is a system of government that includes the national government and a level of subnational governments, such as state and local governments. Each level of government in this system has the ability to make significant decisions, although not completely independently of one another.[2] The development of this system in the United States is thus a division of power among states, the national government, and tribal nations as outlined in the U.S. Constitution and a wide range of court cases. The relationships among local, state, and federal government, while constantly evolving, are much more clearly defined than the relationships between any of these entities and the tribes. Relations among Indian nations, the federal government, and the states have been a shifting target, and deep legal and historical roots that change continually have made it extremely difficult to properly place Indian nations within the federal system of government. For instance, the federal government has recognized tribes as international sovereigns, domestic dependent nations, wards that require protection, and quasi-sovereign governments.[3] Thus federal policies have fluctuated from treating tribes as separate political entities requiring treaties to an attempt to assimilate tribes into the general society by refusing to recognize sovereignty at all.

Lost in the vacillation is the idea that Indian tribal governments and their relations to other governments within the federal system are unique in that their position relative to both the states and the federal government is not derived from the Constitution; rather, tribal governments derive their powers from an inherent right of self-government. This inherent right and the unique relationship of the tribal governments to the federal government has created special problems in defining the role of tribal governments in the federal system, and the ever-changing status of tribal governments has developed historically. For instance, local governments, through "Dillon's Rule," are creatures of the state and derive their power from the state.[4] Therefore, the place of local governments is outlined. The states, like tribal governments, are perpetually defining their relationship with the federal government in terms of state sovereignty and federal supremacy. However, the U.S. Constitution clearly establishes the supremacy of federal law through the supremacy clause and provides for a much clearer resolution of conflicts between states and the federal government. The judicial system developed rules that determine when state powers are preempted. In this sense, the place of states is somewhat settled—they are sovereign, but their laws can be preempted by the national government. The legal status and the relationship between the tribal and the federal government are quite different in that the policy pendulum has historically swung back and forth between federal trusteeship and tribal self-determination. There has been no "Dillon's Rule" or consistently applied constitutional clause to clarify the position of tribal governments within the federal system as there has been for state and local governments. As a result, federal Indian policies have been administered unevenly through different federal administrations, and state governments have never fully understood how they are to relate to tribal nations. Uneven interpretation, implementation, and shifting of Indian policy can be attributed to the fact that Indian nations have historically been in a state of flux. The complexity of the status of Indian tribes is described by the Supreme Court in *McClanahan v. Arizona State Tax Commission:*

It must always be remembered that the various Indian tribes were once independent and sovereign nations, and that their claim to sovereignty long predates that of our own Government. . . . But it is nonetheless still true, as it was in the last century, that the relation of the Indian tribes living within the borders of the United States to the people of the United States has always been an anomalous one and of complex character. . . . not as States, not as nations, not as possessed of the full attributes of sovereignty, but as a separate people with the power of regulating their internal and social relations, and thus far not brought under the laws of the union or of the States within whose limits they reside.[5]

With such a status, it is no wonder that state-tribal relations are generally tenuous—there are no clear rules by which to operate. Therefore, in order to move beyond conflict and begin developing even a basic understanding of the complexities surrounding state-tribal relations, one must first examine the history of tribal relations with the federal government. This background information allows for an understanding of the status of American Indians in their current setting and reasons for intergovernmental conflict. Over time the states have taken the lead from the federal government and have based their behavior and view of tribal governments upon what they have witnessed happening between the many tribal governments and the various institutions based in Washington, D.C. (Congress, Supreme Court, the presidency, and the multitude of federal agencies).

The framework necessary for greater state-tribal cooperation must be found within the existing concepts of federalism and intergovernmental relations (IGR). IGR involves the study of the structure and nature of government relations in the United States within a federal system involving the national government, states, tribes, and other levels of subnational government. The key to intergovernmental relations, then, is interaction between the actors and institutions of government. Intergovernmental relations is consistent with greater state-tribal cooperation and is an appropriate phrase because, despite common misconceptions, the Indian policy environment involves local, state, federal, and tribal governments. As defined by William Anderson, IGR is "an important body of activities or interactions occurring between governmental units of *all* types and levels within the (U.S.) Federal system."[6]

Unfortunately, while various nuances of IGR have been studied extensively, little attention has been paid to modern tribal-government operating systems. This lack of information has impacted the relationship among federal, state, and tribal governments. Because of the unique status of Indian nations, states and federal agencies tend to view tribal governments as so exotic that they elude understanding. Hence the general view that reservation and tribal governments comprise an arena for conflict, a view that reinforces the presumption that trilateral coordination and cooperation are impossible.

FEDERAL-INDIAN RELATIONS

Indian nations have been in an ambiguous state, with differing policy interpretations, implementations, and relations. This uncertainty has deep-rooted legal ramifications in terms of defining or at least delineating the relationship between the federal and tribal governments. Because of the uncertain status of Indian nations, there continue to be differing interpretations by the courts of tribal-state relations. The federal government and Indian nations thus have a complex relationship, which is "in part pre-constitutional and in part extra-constitutional, grounded in three separate, overlapping, and somewhat incompatible doctrines. These doctrines are treaties, the trust relationship, and the plenary power of Congress in Indian affairs."[7]

Federal-Tribal Treaty Relationship

The status of Indian tribes in the United States can be explained by European legal traditions and, subsequently, colonial history. From a historical perspective, American Indians have evolved through discovery, conquest, treaty making, and self-determination. These concepts outline the relationship of Indian tribes to the United States.[8] From a legal perspective, traditions concerning property rights and self-rule date back to the medieval Roman Catholic Church, which was the leading legal and political institution of Western Europe.[9] The church was so dominant that legal scholar Robert Williams has commented that it "had developed and refined a legal tradition which justified denying complete rights of self rule and property to non-Christian peoples . . . ".[10] Ultimately, this Old World concept would pervade the legal framework for Indian and non-Indian relations in the New World. It would further permeate the legal reasoning in three of the most noted cases in American Indian law, the Marshall Trilogy.

Although most federal laws concerning Indian affairs were made after the Declaration of Independence in 1776, Felix Cohen traced the legal history of Indian tribes back to 1532, when Francisco De Victoria, a prominent theologian, lectured on the rights and status of Indian peoples in light of Spain's "discovery" of the New World. Europeans adopted much of De Victoria's lecture on Indian property rights concerning the transfer of land title between Europeans and Indian tribes. His lectures subsequently formed the primary source for the treatment of Indian peoples in international and U.S. law.

Francisco De Victoria had been asked by the emperor of Spain to advise on Spanish rights to land title in the New World. De Victoria concluded that "the aborigines in question were true owners, before the Spaniards came among them, both from the public and the private point of view."[11] According to De Victoria, since the Indians owned the land, neither "discovery" of the continent nor divine right was legally sufficient to establish title. Title to land by discovery, then, could only be legitimated if the property was ownerless. De Victoria theorized that Spain should acquire the Indians' land only with their consent, as expressed through treaties. Treaties were based on several assumptions: 1. That both parties to treaties were sovereign; 2. That the Indian has a transferable title to the land in question; 3. That the acquisition of Indian lands could not be safely left to individual colonists but must be controlled as a governmental monopoly.[12]

These assumptions, as Cohen notes, formed the basis for treaty making with Indian tribes during the early development of the eastern seaboard by European colonists. Colonists in the early years employed treaties as a method of resolving issues related to land, alliance, military partnership, and trade. These treaties, then, implied the recognition of tribal governments and their independent existence, thus rendering them legitimate.[13] These legal documents are, according to Frank Pommersheim, not only the bedrock and cornerstone of tribal sovereignty (however defined), but also of federal- and state-tribal relations.[14]

The treaty making established during the colonial era continued after the war for independence. In the period immediately following the Revolutionary War, tribes were treated as international sovereigns and dealt with on that basis. Treaty making had been left to the individual colonies prior to the Declaration of Independence in 1776, and under the Articles of Confederation colonies (now states) preserved their right to deal with Indian tribes within their boundaries. Indian affairs, however, became a federal matter after the adoption of the U.S. Constitution. By ratifying the Constitution, the states agreed to delegate certain powers to the national government. One of the powers given to the central government was the management of Indian affairs; thus the national government assumed the responsibility of handling Indian affairs through treaties.[15] The principal purpose of treaties, aside from maintaining peace, was of course the transfer of land ownership to the United States. These formal dealings involved cessions of aboriginal lands, boundaries, foreign relations, peace, war, extradition, and the recognition of internal tribal governing powers in return for U.S. protection, trade goods, and hunting and fishing rights.[16] While many of these treaties dealt with the acquisition of Indian land, the very nature of the negotiations indicated that the new U.S. government viewed tribal governments as distinct political entities with a legal status that required treaty making and a government-to-government approach.[17] Treaties, then, pronounced Indian tribes legitimate entities that had indeed developed a system of government. Accordingly, tribal governments were afforded the status of foreign nations through treaty negotiations.

Treaties, then, are not only the cornerstone for a government-to-government relationship, but also, as Pommersheim noted, "they become the closest to a (Federal) constitutional benchmark from which to engage in legal discourse about the nature of tribal sovereignty in a constitutional democracy ... treaties also form the foundation that gives tribal state relations any analytic coherence in the first instance."[18]

Under the treaty-making approach, the status of tribes in the federal system was very clear. However, what had worked well for many years would become clouded, and the status of tribal governments would become less clear as the nation grew and required more territory, and paternalistic forces would push for assimilation of Indians into the white world.

The Trust Relationship

While to modern observers the treaty relationship was a fairly straightforward approach to tribal relations, the status of tribal governments was being questioned during much of our founding period. Unfortunately, much of the questioning centered on how best to integrate tribal governments into the U.S. system in a manner that would be politically satisfactory to an increasingly antagonistic general public. Thus in the early 1820s the Supreme Court was given the responsibility for defining the federal-Indian relationship and the status of Indian nations. The Court first attempted to define the relationship between Indian tribes and the federal government in *Johnson v. Macintosh*.[19] This 1823 case preceded several key decisions that reinforced the "uniqueness" of federal-Indian relations. These cases are known as the Marshall Trilogy.[20]

Chief Justice John Marshall in *Johnson v. McIntosh* created a landlord-tenant relationship between Indian nations and the U.S. government. Although the concept of discovery as theorized by Francisco De Victoria on Indian title to land and property rights resonates in Marshall's decision, Marshall essentially amended De Victoria's theory. According to Marshall, discovery gave land ownership and title to European settlers, but Indians still had the right of occupancy and use. In his decision, Marshall stated:

The rights of the original habitants were, in no instance, entirely disregarded; but were, necessarily, to a considerable extent, impaired. They were admitted to be the rightful occupants of the soil, with a legal as well as just claim to retain possession of it, and use it according to their own discretion; but their rights to complete sovereignty, as independent nations, were necessarily diminished, and their power to dispose of the soil at their own will, to whomever they pleased, was denied by the original fundamental principal, that discovery gave exclusive title to those who made it.[21]

According to the Marshall Court, the "federal government as the ultimate landlord, not only possessed the power to terminate the 'tenancy' of its Indian occupants but also could materially affect the lives of Indians through its control and regulation of land use. With the exercise of power comes responsibility, and *Johnson* constituted a judicially-recognized federal responsibility over Indian affairs."[22] According to Deloria and Lytle, the decision "traded a vested property right for a recognized political right of quasi-sovereignty for the tribes."[23]

Ten years after having placed limitations on tribal sovereignty in Mc-

Intosh, Marshall reinforced the quasi-sovereign status of tribal governments in *Cherokee Nation v. Georgia*. This decision further diminished the sovereign status of tribal governments in relation to the U.S. government. While the ruling implied that tribes were self-sufficient, the Court plainly stated that tribes could not be considered foreign nations (which was a marked shift from the treaty-making period, which did exactly that). The ruling in *Cherokee Nation v. Georgia* relegated tribes to the status of wards in a guardian-ward relationship with the federal government. The Cherokee, Justice Marshall argued, constituted not a "foreign state," but a "state." The Chief Justice declared that the Cherokee

proved the character of a state, as a distinct political society separated from others, capable of managing its own affairs and governing itself . . . Meanwhile they are in a state of pupilage; their relation to the United States resembles that of a ward to his guardian. Indian tribes may be dominated domestic, dependent nations.[24]

In making the decision, Marshall essentially ruled that the federal government had a responsibility for Indian tribes, since "the Indians had looked to the United States government for protection . . . and are completely under the sovereignty of the United States."[25] Again, the shifting of the federal-tribal relationship was well under way, and a new concept emerged that clouds the issue to the present day—that of the "trust relationship." In stating that tribes were dependent nations, the United States had taken on the responsibility of providing for tribes. The trust relationship has been at the center of both federal-tribal and state-tribal relations for quite some time.

In 1832, Samuel Worcester, a missionary who was invited to the Cherokee Nation, was arrested for violating Georgia state law that prohibited non-Cherokee from abiding by tribal law. Worcester was convicted, but when the case was appealed to the Supreme Court, Marshall ruled in Worcester's favor. In *Worcester v. Georgia*, Marshall held that a state could not enforce its laws on Indian lands. Marshall wrote:

The Cherokee Nation, then, is a distinct community, occupying its own territory, with boundaries accurately described, in which the laws of Georgia can have no force, and which the citizens of Georgia have no right to enter, but with the assent of the Cherokees themselves, or in conformity with treaties, and with the acts of congress.[26]

The combination of the decisions in the Marshall Trilogy defined the relationship of Indian nations not only to the federal government, but also to the states. The lines had been drawn. Tribes lost sovereign status relative to the federal government, which now owned the land and maintained a guardian relationship to the tribes. At the same time, the Court preserved tribal sovereignty when it came to dealings with state governments. The cases established that Indian nations, although under the protection of the U.S. government, still had the sovereignty to preclude the states from imposing jurisdictional authority over Indian country as Indian tribes were engaged in the act of self-government.

These three cases form the foundation of the current tribal status, and are critical in understanding federal-Indian relations because they address the rights of Indian tribes as distinct, independent political communities to govern themselves based on treaties and statutes of Congress. Hence Indian tribes have internal power over tribal membership, inheritance, tribal taxation, property, domestic relations, the form of tribal government, laws, and customs. The decisions of the proper tribal government authorities have the force of law.

The issue of federal fiduciary obligation also is established in terms of the trust responsibility. The trust responsibility of the United States is the duty to assist Indians in the protection of their property and rights for natural resources, fish, wildlife, etc., on Indian lands. Finally, the trilogy confirmed that states must have congressional approval before exercising jurisdiction over Indian lands. The general rule is that states have no authority over Indian affairs, tribal government, or reservation lands, except where Congress explicitly grants such authority. Thus the power of the states to regulate relations with Indian nations is delegated power from either the federal government or the Indian nation itself.

Congressional Plenary Power

The authority of Congress to legislate Indian affairs stems from the plenary power doctrine. This doctrine is rooted in the Marshall Trilogy, wherein Indian tribes' status within the U.S. political system was defined as one of dependence on a more powerful nation for protection, thus forming a protectorate/wardship relationship. Protection took the form of guardianship over independence and the defense of tribal sovereignty against outsiders, such as the states. But "protection" took a new meaning in *US v. Kagama* (1886) and *Lone Wolf v. Hitchcock* (1903).

In *Kagama*, the Court established that the power of Congress over Indian nations went beyond regulating commerce as established by the U.S. Constitution. The Court asserted that the tribes' dependent status gave the federal government not just the responsibility of protection, but also power over the tribes. Thus the government's role was one of guardianship, and this role was extended to complete power over Indian affairs because Indians were defenseless and dependent on the government. In dismissing the commerce clause as relevant and extending the power of Congress, the Court stated:

This clause is relied on in the argument in the present case, the proposition being that the statute under consideration is a regulation of commerce with the Indian tribes. But we think it would be a very strained construction of this clause . . . but these Indians are within the geographic limits of the United States. The soil and the people within these limits are under the political control of the government of the United States . . . The power of the General Government over these remnants of a race once powerful, now weak and diminished in numbers, is necessary to their protection.[27]

In *Lone Wolf v. Hitchcock,* the Court upheld the almost unquestioned power of Congress over the tribes. In this ruling, the Court was asked to determine whether Congress was acting in the best interest of the tribes and whether tribal leaders had been deceived in the process leading up to the General Allotment Act (the Dawes Act).

In its ruling, the Court essentially stated that dealing with the tribes was the power of Congress alone, and that political questions were beyond the scope of the Court's power. According to the opinion delivered by Justice White,

Plenary authority over the tribal relations of the Indians has been exercised by Congress from the beginning, and the power has always been deemed a political one, not subject to be controlled by the judicial department of government. We must presume that Congress acted in perfect good faith in the dealings of which complaint is made, and that the legislative branch of the government exercised their best judgement in the premises. In any event, Congress possessed full power in the matter.[28]

Together, the three doctrines—treaties, the trust relationship, and plenary power—established that Indian tribes retained internal sovereignty, although their power over reservation territory and affairs were diminished; that the United States has trust responsibility for Indian tribes; and that Congress has an almost unquestioned legislative plenary authority over matters that concern Indian tribes.[29] Federal Indian policy has developed within this framework, with vestiges of each period coming to the forefront from time to time, thus creating a continuously shifting set of rules for states and tribes to follow.

INDIAN POLICY

Subsequent to these landmark cases, evidence suggests that federal-Indian relations have fluctuated between self-determination and paternalism. In general, federal Indian policy has consisted of numerous failed attempts at indoctrinating native peoples into the larger society. One example has been the shift from assimilation attempts to reorganization efforts.

Assimilation policies of the twentieth century, mostly through The General Allotment Act, did not improve Indian welfare overall; in fact, these policies were disastrous—politically, culturally, and economically. As part of the New Deal effort in the midst of the Great Depression, John Collier, secretary of the Interior under Franklin D. Roosevelt, began working on legislation that would solve the Indian problem and end the policy of allotment.[30] Through the Indian Reorganization Act (IRA) of 1934, Congress prohibited any further allotments of Indian lands and recognized the absolute discretionary power held by the Interior Department over Indian affairs.[31] The IRA also established procedures for the conduct of internal tribal business; these procedures were subject to the discretion of the secretary of the Interior. The Indian Reorganization Act allowed tribes to draft their own constitutions parallel to the U.S. system of governance. Congressional funds for economic development were also made available. The Act was praised for its revival of tribal governments but criticized for being assimilationist, since the government provided tribes with Western-derived political institutions as the model for their governments instead of improving traditional systems.[32] While Western-derived, these governments were, yet again, treated as semi-sovereigns (although not to the extent of the treaty-making period), and the government-to-government approach was reintroduced to federal-tribal relations via the Bureau of Indian Affairs.

Any potential progress that might have come out of the IRA, however, was nullified by Congress through yet another exercise of plenary power. Congress believed that they could "liberate" Indians by terminating the government-to-government federal-Indian relationship and supervising federal Indian programs, such as economic assistance and social services. Under the administration of President Eisenhower, the Indian Termination policy was implemented. Congress further declared it to be the "policy of Congress, as rapidly as possible, to make the Native Americans subject to the same laws and entitled to the same privileges and responsibilities as are applicable to other citizens of the United States."[33]

In the 1950s and early 1960s, congressional support of tribal governments ended with the passage of several termination bills supported largely by Senator Arthur Watkins. These bills were intended to solve the ever-present "Indian problem" by nullifying the federal government's relationship with tribes and integrating their lands and peoples into surrounding states. Congress thereafter terminated its relationship with 109 communities, bands, and tribes. The impact of the Termination policy on Indian tribes was significant. Some of the consequences were the nullification of trust relationship, the imposition of state legislative and judicial jurisdiction, and the virtual abolishment of tribal sovereignty.[34]

The 1960s found the United States in a period of cultural and political awakening. Civil rights were being restored to many Americans and tribal nations began to reassert long-dormant claims for cultural and political autonomy. This movement, coupled with apparent mismanagement by the BIA, led President Lyndon Johnson to begin a policy shift back toward tribal independence. In 1969, Johnson created the National Council on Indian Opportunity in order for Indian issues to be better heard by federal officials.[35] Federal Indian policy once again swung toward tribal autonomy. As part of the War on Poverty, tribal governments were allowed to receive federal social-welfare and economic-development program funding.

In 1970 President Nixon announced the official federal Indian policy of self-determination. Nixon essentially denounced the policy of termination and said that this policy had severely damaged the trust relationship between the tribes and the federal government. "The practical results have been clearly harmful in the few instances in which termination actually has been tried. The removal of the Federal Trusteeship responsibility has produced considerable disorientation among the affected Indians and has left them unable to relate to the myriad of Federal, state, and local assistance efforts. Their economic and social condition has often been worse after termination than it was before."[36] In his address, Nixon also announced that "the time has come to break decisively with the past and to create the conditions for a new era in which the Indian future is determined by Indian acts and decisions." [37]

Contemporary Indian policy and relations are predicated on the philosophical foundation laid by Nixon. On January 4, 1975, Congress implemented the Indian Self-Determination and Education Assistance Act of 1975, which permits tribes to assume control of many federal programs on Indian reservations. The Act gives express authority to the secretaries of the Interior and Health and Human Services to contract with, and make grants to, Indian tribes and other Indian organizations for the delivery of federal services. The Act reflects a fundamental philosophical change concerning the administration of Indian affairs. The federal government funds tribal programs, but the programs are controlled and operated by the tribes themselves. The Indian Financing Act, also passed in 1974, provided grants and loans to help Native Americans utilize and manage their own financial resources for reservation development. Cultural integrity was taken into consideration with the passage of the Indian Religious Freedom Act of 1978.

The American Indian Policy Review Commission was also established and charged with the responsibility of reviewing existing federal policy on Indian affairs and making recommendations to improve Indian policy in subjects such as tribal government, economic development, education, and health.

Congress's present approach to tribal governments is to acknowledge and promote tribal self-determination. The federal government's relationship with tribes today is a trust relationship. As legislation concerning Indian affairs changes, this relationship continues to develop. The federal government under current law is responsible for protecting Native American lands and resources, providing social services such as health and educational benefits, and maintaining tribal autonomy. These rights and benefits are owed to tribes as a result of promises made by the federal government in return for the cession of more than 97 percent of Indian land to non-Indians.[38]

Tribal governments, as sovereigns, receive their authority to operate from their own people, not from the Constitution. Tribal governments are recognized by Congress on a limited government-to-government basis and no longer considered complete wards of the federal government. As such, "Tribes possess the inherent sovereignty to exercise all governmental power unless extinguished by treaty or congressional legislation or unless it is a power that is inconsistent with the tribes' dependent status."[39] Practically, this means that tribes maintain, with some limitations, the authority to structure their own governments, to administer justice, regulate domestic relations, manage and develop their lands and resources, conduct businesses, and tax individuals and commercial enterprises.[40]

From the early 1980s through the present, Indian policy has begun to shift once again. A number of legislative acts, such as the Tribal Self-government Act of 1988 and the Indian Tribal Economic Development and Contract Encouragement Act of 2000, pushed the era of self-determination to new heights and aimed toward an era of true self-government. At the forefront of the current movement was former president Bill Clinton, who told tribal leaders gathered in Washington that "together, we can open the greatest era of cooperative understanding and respect among our people ever."[41] Clinton followed through with his promise by issuing numerous executive orders that directed federal agencies to treat tribal nations on a government-to-government basis.

Unfortunately, a Republican Congress and conservative Supreme Court have made moves that undermine many of the gains made since the early part of the self-determination era. Many Court decisions, for example, have tended to support state sovereignty over tribal sovereignty when the two were at odds. Such decisions have led leading Indian scholar David Wilkins to note that

the policy ambivalence evident in the conflicting goals of sometimes recognizing tribal self-determination and sometimes seeking to terminate that governing status has lessened only slightly over time. Tribal Nations and their citizens find that their efforts to exercise inherent sovereignty are rarely unchallenged.[42]

The comment by Wilkins is mirrored by Francis Prucha, who feels that federal-Indian relations have been marked by conflict and paternalism from the colonial era to the present. In other words, little has changed.[43] It is within this context that states and tribes are being asked to forge new partnerships.

SUMMARY

The U.S. federal system of government consists of three primary parts—the national, state, and local governments. Charters, constitutions, and court decisions form the basis for authority and relations at each level of government. Tribal governments, however, were originally not part of this system. As a result, they were initially dealt with on the basis of international law. Formal government relations were established through treaties and agreements. Because of their changing legal and political status, Indian nations have been treated as international sovereigns, domestic dependent nations, and quasi-sovereign governments. In the course of defining the legal and political status of these unique enclaves within the U.S. political system, federal-Indian relations have evolved through protectorate and guardianship to the present-day trust relationship, which is a less dictatorial form of the original trust relationship developed via the Marshall Trilogy. The modern trust relationship is based on a combination of international law, treaties, federal judicial decisions, legislation, and presidential decrees. The modern trust relationship, when coupled with the push for self-determination, relies more heavily upon tribal autonomy. At the same time, paternalistic tendencies have been a part of dealings with tribal nations from the very beginning of our nation. The combination of the federal trust relationship, paternalism, and tribal self-government form a complex backdrop for examining ways to improve state-tribal relations.

NOTES

1. Ryser, "When Tribes and States Collide," p. 5.
2. Nice and Fredrickson, *Intergovernmental Relations*.
3. Deloria, Jr., and Lytle, *Nations Within*, pp. 234–64.
4. Deil S. Wright, *Understanding Intergovernmental Relations* (Pacific Grove, CA: Brooks/Cole Publishing Company, 1988), p. 14.
5. *McClanahan v. Arizona State Tax Commission,* 411 U.S. 164, 93 S.Ct. 1257, 36 L.Ed. 2d 129 (1973).
6. William Anderson, *Understanding Intergovernmental Relations in Review* (Minneapolis, MN: University of Minnesota Press, 1960), p. 3.
7. Pommersheim, "Tribal State Relations," p. 239.
8. Robert A. Williams, Jr., *The American Indian in Western Legal Thought: The Discourses of Conquest* (New York: Oxford University Press, 1990).
9. Ibid.
10. Ibid.

11. Felix S. Cohen, *The Handbook of Federal Indian Law* (1942), pp. 46–47.
12. Ibid.
13. William C. Canby, Jr., *American Indian Law in a Nutshell* (St. Paul, MN: West Publishing Company, 1988).
14. Pommersheim, "Tribal State Relations."
15. Canby, *American Indian Law*.
16. Ibid.
17. David H. Getches, Charles F. Wilkinson, and Robert A. Williams, Jr., *Federal Indian Law: Cases and Material*, 3d ed (St. Paul, MN: West Publishing Company, 1993), p. 83.
18. Pommersheim, "Tribal State Relations," p. 242.
19. *Johnson v. McIntosh*, 21 U.S. (8 Wheat.) 543 (1823).
20. Canby, *American Indian Law*.
21. *Johnson v. McIntosh* (1823).
22. Vine Deloria, Jr., and Clifford M. Lytle, *American Indians, American Justice* (Austin, TX: University of Texas Press, 1983), pp. 26–27.
23. Ibid., p. 4.
24. *Cherokee Nation v. Georgia*, 30 U.S. (5 Pet.) 1, 8 L.Ed. 25 (1831).
25. Ibid.
26. *Worcester v. Georgia*, 31 U.S. (6 Pet.) 515, 8 L.Ed. 483 (1832).
27. *United States v. Kagama*, 118 U.S. 375, S.Ct. 1109, 30 L.Ed. 228 (1886).
28. *Lone Wolf v. Hitchcock*, 187 U.S. 553, 23 S.Ct. 216, 47 L.Ed. 299 (1903).
29. Getches, Wilkinson, and Williams, *Federal Indian Law*.
30. Kenneth Philp, *John Collier's Crusade for Indian Reform* (Tucson, AZ: University of Arizona Press, 1978).
31. *Indian Reorganization Act*, 25 U.S.C.A., p. 461–78.
32. Deloria, Jr., and Lytle, *American Indians*.
33. Richard L. Worsnop, "Native Americans," *CQ Researcher*, vol. 2 (8 May 1992), p. 397.
34. Wilkinson and Biggs, "Termination Policy," pp. 92–93.
35. Wilkins, *American Indian Politics*, p. 222.
36. Monroe Price, *Law and the American Indian: Readings, Notes, and Cases* (Indianapolis, IN: Bobbs-Merrill Co., 1973), p. 599.
37. Ibid., p. 597.
38. O'Brien, *Tribal Governments*, pp. 261–62.
39. Ibid., pp. 276–77.
40. Canby, *American Indian Law*.
41. President William Clinton, Speech, 29 April 1994, http://www.his.gov/PublicInfo/publicAffairs/pressreleases/pressrelease1994/presmes.asp.
42. Wilkins, *American Indian Politics*, p. 118.
43. Francis Paul Prucha, *The Great Father: The United States Government and the American Indians* (Lincoln, NE: University of Nebraska Press, 1984).

CHAPTER 3

Sovereignty and the State-Tribal Relationship

One of the clearest themes involving Indian sovereignty in the last two centuries has been the continuous struggle by the states to assert control over Indian reservations. The pace of the struggle, the form that it takes and the forum in which the struggle occurs have changed from decade to decade ... the repeated efforts by the state governments to extend their power and the standards over Indian country within their borders ... is a process which has been influenced by economic, moral and jurisprudential considerations, probably in that order.[1]

The history of state-tribal relations has always been one of confrontation. The relationship between Indian nations and the federal government is predicated on the inherent sovereignty of tribes. Theoretically, this means that because of their treaty relationship with the federal government, Indian tribes have a higher status than states, and the only means by which states can exercise jurisdiction over an Indian tribe is through Congress (exercising the plenary power). For instance, in *Native American Church v. Navajo Tribal Council*, a federal court stated that "Indian tribes are not states. They have a status higher than that of states. They are subordinate and dependent nations possessed of all powers as such only to the extent that they have been expressly required to surrender them by the superior sovereign, the United States."[2]

The tribal-state legal relationship can be better understood by examining the *Worcester v. Georgia* decision. In this case, the Supreme Court ruled that the state of Georgia could not enforce its laws on the Cherokee Indian Reservation. The Court found that states had no authority to pass laws that interfered with the federal-tribal relationship. Federal law and inherent tribal sovereignty ruled out any state control over Indian tribes.[3] However, as trustee of Indian nations, the federal court system has often demonstrated a conservative interpretation of the status of Indian nations. In Indian matters, conflicts within the federal system have had much to do with the federal government's responsibility to meet treaty obligations. Historically, the pressures of manifest destiny and the nature of the federal system influenced the way the government dealt with Indian nations. Federal Indian law is subject to fluctuating political conditions and the interest of the larger polity.

Since the colonial era and the advent of the American government, the status of Indian nations has been the subject of litigation and federal legislation. The current jurisdictional framework normally encompasses a trilateral tension between the federal government, the states, and the tribes, and an ongoing assertion by each body of jurisdictional authority over Indian reservations. This assertion normally involves interests such as natural resources found on Indian reservations, taxation, gaming, criminal jurisdiction, and more. States justify their position by pointing to the fact that Indian reserves are not extraterritorial; instead, they are within state boundaries. To complicate the relationship even further, portions of many tribal lands are held in fee by non-Indians. This checkerboard land ownership pattern presents a jurisdictional maze of non-Indians and tribal members living next to one another—with authority over them falling to different entities, often on an issue-by-issue basis. In addition, due to its concomitant role in Indian affairs, the federal government often finds itself thrown into the confusing question of who has authority over particular issues or programs under changing situations and conditions.

In this chapter the various pieces of legislation that have clouded the issue of state tribal jurisdiction and sovereignty are highlighted. The Dawes Act, Public Law 280, and The Indian Gaming Regulatory Act are but a few. The chapter also includes several cases that involve tribal-state relations and are cited to accentuate the differing strands of decisions and the still evolving status of Indian tribes within the American political system. Federal Indian law and policy still present challenges to the U.S. Supreme Court. The existing complexity and ambiguity is perpetuated in a series of cases concerning tribal-state relations decided by the U.S. Supreme Court. These cases are evidence of the problems that stem from differing makeup (i.e., checkerboard land ownership, PL 280 reservations) and status of tribal lands, and the attempts of both tribes and states to assert jurisdictional authority over natural resources, property rights, and any other areas within the boundaries of the reservation.

CONGRESSIONAL CHANGES TO THE STATE-TRIBAL RELATIONSHIP

Indian tribes are pre-constitutional—they do not derive their powers from the U.S. Constitution, and hence, are inherent sovereigns. This has not stopped the U.S. government from assuming responsibility for tribal nations and from acting on their behalf. Since the beginnings of the Union, relations between the United States and Indian tribes have been justified partly by the constitutional powers of the president. The two sources of presidential power with regard to Indian tribes are the treaty-making powers under Article II section 2 and the war power as commander in chief. Both of these constitutionally based powers were used in the U.S.-Indian relationship in the early days of the Republic.

Another source of governmental responsibility for Indian tribes is the authority of Congress. First, Congress has much authority under the Commerce Clause, Article I, section 8 of the Constitution. The second congressional source of authority is the plenary power that is found in the "Marshall trilogy" in which the dependent status of Indian nations rendered them in need of protection, supplied by Congress in its role as guardian. However, the guardianship theory has been expanded to absolute control over Indian affairs (*U.S. v. Kagama* and *Lone Wolf v. Hitchcock*). Hence, Indian tribes (as legal entities) exist at the mercy of the U.S. Congress. This has meant that whenever Congress has decided to change its view of the trust relationship and corresponding policy, the rules surrounding the relationship between states and tribes have necessarily changed. Congressional actions have led to many such changes over time and have made working toward state-tribal relations very problematic.

The General Allotment Act (Dawes Act)

The General Allotment Act, better known as the Dawes Act, was passed in 1887. The Act had two primary purposes—neither of which was good for preserving tribal sovereignty. The first stated goal of the Dawes Act was to assimilate tribes into mainstream society. If there is any question that the Dawes Act was intended to strip tribes of their identity, one need only look to the words of President Theodore Roosevelt, who referred to the Act and the policy of allotment as "a mighty pulverizing engine to break up the tribal mass."[4] While the reservation system had once been pushed as a method for assimilation and the breaking up of tribalism, it was apparent that cultures and traditional ways had remained largely intact. It was believed that this was partly due to the fact that there was no pride of land ownership and the corresponding ability to work one's own land for sustenance and profit. In other words, well-intentioned reformers believed that Indians were not being assimilated into society simply because they were not being introduced to the ways of non-Indians. The Act took communal tribal land and broke it up into smaller pieces that were to be distributed to individual Indians who agreed to adopt a European-based farming existence. In order to ensure that a transition into this existence took place, these individual plots were placed in trust and could not be sold for 25 years.[5] Any "surplus" lands not granted to individual tribal members could be granted to non-Indians. This allowed for the infusion of many non-Indians into Indian country—supposedly to aid in the reeducation of Indians in the ways of the "American." To further accelerate the assimilation into society, Indian-owned plots were often separated by privately held land (fee lands), which created the checkerboarding phenomenon that plagues many reservations today and continues to cause jurisdictional confusion.

An unspoken purpose of the Dawes Act was the fulfillment of manifest destiny and the need for additional land. To many observers, the Act was the result of political pressure applied by land speculators and western settlers. Rather than looking out for any tribal interest, these people simply wanted to obtain Indian land and would go along with any guise to get it. While the Act was promoted as being in the best interest of the tribes (thus not in violation of the trust responsibility), not all members of Congress agreed. Prior to the passage of the General Allotment Act, a House minority report coming out of the Indian Affairs Committee stated the following:

The real aim of this bill is to get the Indian lands and open them up to settlement. The provisions for the apparent benefit of the Indian are but a pretext to get at his lands and occupy them. . . . If this were done in the name of greed, it would be bad enough; but to do so in the name of humanity, and under the cloak of an ardent desire to promote the Indian's welfare by making him like ourselves whether he will or not, is infinitely worse.[6]

Despite the small opposition, the Act passed and tribal lands were broken up, with a tremendous amount of land being lost in the process. Not only was the total acreage diminished, those lands that remained in tribal possession were often commingled with land held by non-Indians who fell beyond tribal jurisdiction and under the arm of the state. The checkerboarding and commingling is one of the hardest issues to tackle when states and tribes sit down and attempt to cooperate. Hence, in this case, state-tribal relations have been hampered somewhat by the plenary power of Congress.

The McCarren Amendment

The changing tribal, state, and federal relationship can be understood using the Winters doctrine as an example. This doctrine established the reserving of water for Indian tribes. The doctrine basically states that Indian water rights are products of federal law and hence preempt state water laws from being imposed on Indians. Moreover, the doctrine established that the time of the water right was perfected at the time of a treaty being signed or a reservation being established. This is particularly crucial in most of the West where the doctrine of prior appropriation reigns. Winters made it so that reservation water rights took priority over almost all state-established appropriations, which tended to take place much later than the creation of the reservations. The doctrine should have clarified any question surrounding state-tribal water rights and was in line with the federal trust responsibility—tribes had prior water rights and these rights were federal rights that could only be challenged by suing the federal government.

In 1952 Congress passed the McCarren Amendment. The United States, under the doctrine of sovereign immunity, is protected from being sued unless it consents to being sued. Under the McCarren Amendment, the government allowed limited waiver of this protection in water rights litigation.[7] Since the government could now be sued, it was reasoned that since federal Indian law and Indian water rights fall under the jurisdiction of the government, these water rights could now be litigated in state courts. Not surprisingly, water rights litigated in western state courts generally resulted in decisions that went against the tribes and for the state. This was demonstrated in the *San Carlos Apache Tribe v. Arizona* when the Court held that the state courts are the proper forum to adjudicate Indian water rights, and it also indicated that the McCarren Amendment waived the sovereign immunity of Indian tribes.[8] From a tribal perspective, another unfavorable court decision that expanded the McCarren Amendment is *Colorado River Conservation District v. United States*.[9] Once again, the Court concluded that state courts have jurisdiction over Indian water rights under the Amendment. While the Court insisted that the federal government still had a fiduciary responsibility, and that state courts could not violate the Winters doctrine, it was clear that the McCarren Amendment had allowed for state challenges to tribal water rights and sovereignty. Water rights is one of the more hotly contested issues of state-tribal relations and can, in many cases, be a topic that precludes states and tribes from cooperating in other areas.

Public Law 280

Public Law 280 (PL 280) was enacted in August 1953.[10] It mandatorily transferred civil and criminal jurisdiction over reservation Indians to five specific states and provided the mechanism for the transfer of jurisdiction to other states. The five original states were California, Minnesota, Nebraska, Oregon, and Wisconsin. Alaska was added in 1958. PL 280 was enacted because "assimilation was cheaper for the federal government and preferred by states that disliked the presence of an Indian sovereignty within their borders."[11]

Public Law 83–280 is a companion of the termination policy that marked the 1950s. Rather than enter into treaties with tribes or allow them to continue to function as domestic dependent sovereigns, the thought of the times was to finally integrate tribes into mainstream society once and for all. With this in mind, the termination period and PL 280 had the intent of getting the federal government out of the "Indian problem." Thus civil and criminal jurisdiction was transferred to the states and the law was extended to all other states willing to accept jurisdiction over Indian reservations.[12]

While Congress viewed PL 280 as a compromise between complete termination of a tribe's recognition and the perceived need for societal integration, the law was not fully embraced by either of the parties impacted by PL 280—the states and tribes. Despite several states assuming jurisdiction under PL 280 (i.e., California, Oregon, Wisconsin, Iowa, etc.), the law had several major flaws. A majority of the states did not accept PL 280, as they could neither receive federal funding nor tax Indian reservations for generating revenue. In other words, they were being asked to assume jurisdiction without receiving any resources with which to do so. The federal government also kept the authority to control trust lands, and states were restricted from abrogating treaty rights. Indian tribes naturally objected to the law, as they were not provided consent when a state opted to assert jurisdiction. Congress did not even consult tribes before the passage of PL 280.[13]

PL 280 was amended by Congress in 1968 to provide that the states could thereafter assume jurisdiction over Indian land only if the Indians involved consented to the assumption. This provision was critical as it marked a change from the assimilationist perspective of PL 280 and state jurisdiction to a perspective of self-determination and assistance. Rather than force tribes to lose sovereignty and fall under control of the state, tribes were allowed to choose when state-run programs were in the best interest of their members. Unfortunately, the consent provision was not made retroactive and earlier assumptions of state jurisdiction, made against the will of tribal governments, were not altered.[14]

PL 280 was clearly a federal action that changed the state-tribal relationship. Stripping tribes of jurisdiction was a clear deterioration of tribal sovereignty and made the state into the enemy in many cases. That states were able to pick and choose where they were going to assume authority has led to a certain amount of confusion. There has also been a fair amount of retrocession where the states, finding programs to be prohibitively costly, have returned jurisdiction to the United States (tribes are not given a similar "out" when state jurisdiction does not appear to be in their interests).[15] With full assumption, partial assumption, and retrocession, PL 280 has created a jurisdictional maze that hampers state-tribal cooperative efforts in the current era. Moreover, the forced deterioration of tribal sovereignty and the ready intrusion by some states has created a lasting sense of mistrust between states and tribes that must be overcome in any attempts to work together for mutual gain.

Indian Gaming Regulatory Act

One of the most recent federal actions that takes the U.S. government largely out of its relationship with tribes and thrusts Indian nations directly into a relationship with the states (a radical departure from Worcester) is the Indian Gaming Regulatory Act of 1988. The Act allows for tribal gaming as long as it is not in violation of federal law or was not expressly prohibited by state law or policy. In order to engage in gaming enterprises, however, the tribe is forced to enter into a gaming compact with the state. Needless to say, this takes away a great deal of sovereignty relative to state governments—the tribe must, in essence, get state permission before opening up a casino. To its credit, the U.S. government did provide some oversight and the Act allowed the federal government to intervene in the compacting process if it became apparent that the state was not bargaining in good faith. Tribes were allowed to sue the states in federal court and ask for a remedy to the impasse. In 1996, however, this oversight was removed by the Supreme Court in *Seminole Tribe v. Florida*. The Court ruled that Congress did not have the authority to force states to waive their sovereign immunity and that tribes could not sue states without state consent.[16] In other words, tribes could no longer sue states for failing to bargain in good faith over a gaming compact—any impasse has to be resolved by the Secretary of the Interior at his/her discretion. The power of the state over tribal affairs was increased and the inherent sovereignty of the tribes was diminished.

The Indian Gaming Regulatory Act has had both positive and negative results when it comes to tribal self-determination and relations with state governments. Increased revenues have allowed some tribes to internally fund several programs and generally improve the living conditions for many of their members. The surplus funds coming from successful gaming enterprises have also allowed a handful of tribes to become more viable political forces at the state, local, and even federal levels.[17] The money has allowed some, such as the Mashantucket Pequot, to become such viable forces that leading American Indian advocate LaDonna Harris once commented that in Connecticut "the tribe drives the state."[18]

While there are isolated cases of tribes gaining political power when dealing with state government, this is hardly a universal condition. The Indian Gaming Regulatory Act, especially with the *Seminole Tribe v. Florida* changes, has increasingly led to tension between states and tribes as they try to negotiate gaming compacts. As inherent sovereigns, tribes feel that no such negotiation should be necessary and are frustrated by state stalling tactics. The states, for their part, hold most of the cards since the federal courts can no longer be asked to resolve conflict. States can hold out and pressure tribes into accepting compacts that give a very large percentage of the proceeds to the states. States can even attempt to change existing compacts. Wisconsin, for example, signed compacts with eleven different tribes who agreed to pay the state $350,000 per year. By 1998 Governor Tommy Thompson had seen how lucrative gaming really was and decided that tribes would now have to pay closer to $25 million under new compacts.[19] Such conflict strikes at sovereignty and spills over into other areas. When the state and tribe are in the middle of a heated debate over gaming, it is often difficult for law enforcement officials, educators, or environmental managers to separate out their particular issues and make progress toward mutually beneficial cooperative agreements.

JUDICIAL CHANGES TO THE STATE-TRIBAL RELATIONSHIP

Despite the legal framework established by *Worcester v. Georgia* in state-tribal relations, the history of tribal-state relations has been one of legal confrontation. Unfortunately, courts and Congress are not always working together and they often send mixed messages for states and tribes to try and interpret. Beginning in the 1960s, congressional policies, such as amending PL 280 to allow for tribal consent, have often favored Indian self-determination (which allowed Indian tribes to win in both the political and legal arena). Many recent Court decisions, however, have been made in favor of states (obviating the *Worcester* decision). Unfortunately, there has not been any consistency and the Court has tended to follow the historical lead of Congress's ever-changing positions, and the result is confusion.

Initial Court decisions regarding Indians tended to be fairly clear and established clean lines of authority. Examples include *Kagama,* which established congressional plenary power, *Worcester,* which provided for state exclusion from the affairs of Indian nations, and *United States v. McBratney* (1881), which stated that states have complete criminal jurisdiction over non-Indians who commit crimes against non-Indians within reservation bounds.[20] While an abrogation of the sovereign right to govern territory, *McBratney* laid out clear jurisdictional lines. Unfortunately, many cases in the twentieth century were more ambiguous and often led to greater jurisdictional confusion between states and tribes instead of resolving any questions.

Let us now look at several U.S. Supreme Court cases that illustrate that tribal sovereignty has slowly been eroded and replaced by state authority, only to be restored—this time at the hands of the Court rather than Congress. While some of the cases appear to be protective of Indian rights and tribal sovereignty, they were actually moving toward state rights by gradually establishing new precedent and introducing new language to the area of state-tribal law. Then, just as quickly, the Court would rule for the tribes. The Court has been less predictable than Congress and the losers have been the states and tribes who attempt to find a stable environment in which to operate.

While the landmark case *Worcester v. Georgia* reaffirmed the *total* exclusion of state authority on Indian reservations, the Supreme Court has consistently allowed states to have a degree of jurisdictional authority within Indian country. Although the Court does seem conscious of the idea of tribal self-government, the concept of tribal sovereignty has slowly been displaced by ambiguity. In 1959's *Williams v. Lee,* a Navajo defendant had been sued in state court by a non-Indian store owner for transactions that had occurred on the Navajo Reservation. The Supreme Court ruled that the state infringed on the right of self-government.[21] The Court precluded the state of Arizona from infringing on Indian tribal sovereignty but inadvertently created the infringement test. The test holds that state laws may not undermine the authority of the tribe or intrude on reservation residents' ability to make their own laws and be governed by them. In other words, the ground was being laid for the possibility that state actions that impact a tribe might be allowable as long as they do not impede the right of self-government. Such was the case in *Organized Village of Kake v. Egan,* decided only three years after Williams.[22]

In *Warren Trading Post v. Arizona Tax Commission* (1965), the Supreme Court precluded the state of Arizona from taxing the gross receipts of a trading post owned by a non-Indian on the Navajo Reservation. The Court had reversed direction again (only three years after the ruling in the Village of Kake) and protected sovereignty by ignoring the infringement test and basing its ruling on federal preemption. Preemption in federal Indian law holds that Congress has the legislative authority to control what happens on Indian reservations. In deciding the case, the Court commented that the businesses of Indian trading "seem so fully in hand that no room remains for state laws imposing additional burdens upon traders."[23] With the Court moving back and forth over a short six-year span, when did jurisdiction fall to tribes, and when did it fall to the state? The law was anything but clear.

The setting would continue to shift with 1973's *McClanahan v. Arizona Tax Commission.*[24] This case clearly indicates a trend away from tribal sovereignty. Although the Court ruled that the state of Arizona could not collect state income tax on income earned on the reservation, the Court ruled that state laws could be enforced on the reservation if there were no interference in the conduct of tribal self-government and if non-Indians were involved. They utilized the infringement test from *Williams* and found that it had no application in this case. The more damaging blow came in the language the Court used to describe tribal sovereignty in general. The ruling read, in part:

> the trend has been away from the idea of inherent sovereignty as a bar to state jurisdiction and toward reliance on federal pre-emption . . . the modern cases thus tend to avoid reliance on platonic notions of Indian sovereignty and look instead to the applicable treaties and statutes which define the limits of state power . . . The Indian sovereignty doctrine is relevant, then, not because it provides a definitive resolution of the issue in this suit, but because it provides a backdrop against which the applicable treaties and federal statutes must be read.[25]

In other words, sovereignty was not to be considered a guiding principle—merely a "backdrop."

While the Court moved back toward protecting sovereignty with a renewed vision in 1980's *White Mountain Apache Tribe v. Bracker*[26] with a rearticulation of the infringement test, the pattern of vacillation on the issue of state versus tribal jurisdiction had been established. The establishment of jurisdictional guidelines was a shifting target, and either side could go to the courts and hope that they would change their minds—something they had proven was a distinct possibility. Thus the courts reinforced the litigious and adversarial relationship between tribes and states rather than clarifying the relationship so that cooperative efforts might begin. The status of Indian tribes within the United States and their relations with the states have required the balancing of interests in an atmosphere of trilateral tension in tribal, state, and federal government relations. This balancing has resulted in a continuous shifting of state rights and tribal rights by either Congress or the courts.

Currently, relations are affected by misunderstanding, mistrust, and uncertainty. However, some tribes and states have instituted non-adversarial means of dispute resolution in IGR.[27] Unfortunately, tribal-state relations continue to be strained, even in times of voluntary negotiations and deliberations. As W. Dale Mason has noted, there are three main sources that contribute to the negative condition of tribal-state relations. First, constitutional ambiguity complicates relations. That is, the Constitution does not directly mention tribes, tribal relations, or Indian issues. Second, jurisdictional disputes concerning citizenship and/or tribal affiliation of individuals hinder tribal-state negotiations. Questions arising from both Indians living off reservations and non-Indians living on reservations under state jurisdiction present considerable problems for deliberations (as we have seen, congressional actions and court decisions have not helped this at all). Finally, jurisdictional matters and ownership of resources found in geographic areas over which both tribes and states claim jurisdiction continue to cause conflict.[28] While the Tenth Circuit Court's decision in *Native American Church v. Navajo Tribal Council* (1959) mentioned that tribes shall enjoy "a status higher than states,"[29] states continue to assert dominance. With tribes claiming sovereignty, and states claiming supremacy, there have been problems. Implicit in the *Native American Church* ruling is the notion that tribes and states should operate on an equal footing under the law. However, "One of the most divisive intergovernmental conflicts in the history of the United States has occurred between state governments and Indian tribes."[30] Rather than cooperative negotiation, this divisiveness has given way to litigation. There are numerous state and federal court cases that have been impediments to the existence of cooperative and productive state-tribal relations. Most of these disputes fall into three main categories: fishing and/or hunting rights, land jurisdiction matters, and water and natural resource issues and conflicts. These three elements can be effectively analyzed through the lens of various judicial cases. Accordingly, which party (tribes or government) attained victory through litigation seems irrelevant. The point here is that jurisdictional disputes between tribes and states have occurred that have not been resolved outside of the courtroom; this has led to increasingly negative relations. Litigation rather than cooperation and negotiation has historically been the norm, and tensions have continued to rise—making future negotiation that much less likely.

Hunting and Fishing Rights

The issue of fishing and hunting is a sensitive one in tribal-governmental relations. The often fragile balance between the hunting traditions and rights of the indigenous and the government's duty and obligation to sustain, protect, and monitor wildlife and commerce issues arising from hunting and fishing often leads to conflict in the form of litigation. As such, disputes between tribes and states in the areas of hunting and fishing can be viewed as an "ideological" jurisdictional matter. *Puyallup Tribe v. Washington Gaming Department* (1977) involved a protest by the Puyallup Tribe of the state of Washington that challenged the Washington Gaming Department's legal right to regulate fishing both on and off the reservation. The Washington Gaming Department prevailed when the Supreme Court stated that the state has an interest in regulating fishing both on and off the reservation pursuant to conservation concerns.[31] Similarly, *People v. Frank*, a case arising out of the state of California, involved the selling of fish by Indians off reservations. The California Appellate Court found that strict laws dealing with fishing and the selling of fish apply to Indians when they are off reservations.[32] A similar case, *Donahue v. Justice Court* (1971), was an appeal to a California court attempting to prohibit the Klamath-Trinity Judicial District of Humboldt County from prosecuting an appellant, Donahue, who was charged with fishing with a net larger than allowed by law (which is in violation of California Fish and Game Code Sections 8603 and 8686) within the boundaries of the Hoopa Indian Reservation. Citing Public Law 280, the court found that Donahue (since he was an Indian) couldn't be deprived of rights and privileges guaranteed under charters and treaties.[33] Many other court cases, both state and federal, relating to hunting and fishing rights and privileges can be discussed and analyzed in order to show how jurisdictional disputes between tribes and states have manifested themselves in judicial battles. Cases such as *Confederated Salish and Kootenai Tribes v. Montana, State of Montana v. Shook,* and *U.S. v. Washington* illustrate how jurisdictional disputes between tribes and states over hunting and fishing rights have become major judicial battles. The point is that adversarial approaches are far more common than negotiation when it comes to hunting and fishing rights and regulations.

Land Jurisdiction Matters

As stated above, another environmentally based origin of tribal-state litigation deals with land rights and jurisdictional issues. Federally recognized tribes often find themselves at odds with various locales (counties, municipalities, etc.) and states that seek to diminish the scope of Indian-owned land for purposes of expanding their sphere of jurisdiction. Two relatively recent cases involving land rights and jurisdictional issues of federally recognized tribes help to illustrate negative tribal-state relations. *Idaho et al. v. Coeur d'Alene Tribe of Idaho et al.* (1997) involved an Indian tribe in the state of Idaho that was seeking injunctive relief from the judicial system for issues pertaining to land rights. The tribe filed this federal action against the state of Idaho, various state agencies, and numerous state officials in their *individual capacities.* At the core of this case is the fact that the Eleventh Amendment asserts that states cannot have suits brought against them by Indians. The tribe sought an exemption (under *Young*) in which tribes could sue individuals of the state in their individual capacities. The court denied the applicability of *Young.*[34] Hence, this case illustrates poor relations over land jurisdiction issues but also concerning conflict resolution between tribes and states (whether tribes can bring suits against states and the like).

The 2001 U.S. District Court case of *The Canadian St. Regis Band of Mohawk Indians v. State of New York* also shows conflict in jurisdictional matters through litigation. This case involves a land claim brought against the state of New York government by the Mohawk Indians. The tribe claims that, under a nineteenth-century treaty, they are entitled to a variety of lands being used by the state of New York. The court found that New York was in violation of the Non-intercourse Act, but decisions relating to all other aspects of the case were in favor of the state of New York.[35]

As with game and wildlife, litigation has been a common theme for land-based jurisdictional disputes.

Natural Resource Disputes

Water rights litigation is a fairly common theme throughout the nation, and it is particularly common in the West. One such case was *Navajo Nation v. U.S., State of Arizona*. The Navajo Nation sought a declaration of rights for use of the Little Colorado River. The tribe cited treaties and other federal statutes in their defense. The court found that Arizona had "disclaimed" its rights, even water rights, when the issue concerned Indians.[36] Such a ruling, over something as precious as water, undoubtedly made for increased tension between the state of Arizona and the Navajo Nation. Many tribes and state governments are deeply involved in litigation concerning jurisdictional issues. Overcoming the scars left by costly court battles—and the initial mindset that leans toward litigation over negotiation in the first place—will be critical if states and tribes are to ever make greater use of cooperative water quality agreements.

CONCLUSION

The history of tribal-state relations has been one of confrontation in the states' struggle to assert jurisdiction over Indian reservations. Until 1940, no state had authority on Indian reservations. In subsequent years, with the beginning of the termination era, several states were given jurisdiction of criminal matters on Indian reserves. The extent of the granted jurisdiction in these cases, however, was far less than that of Public Law 280. PL 280 essentially took criminal and civil jurisdiction on Indian reservations from the tribes (or the federal government) and gave it to the states. Although many states have declined to exercise their authority in the two areas, mainly for financial reasons, some Indian reserves were and continue to be subject to PL 280.

In some ways, the relationship between tribal, state, and federal governments is similar to that of any governments that deal with overlapping territorial jurisdiction and resource competition. However, tribal governments have a unique status within the American political system unlike that of state governments. Herein lies the source of much conflict and misunderstanding. Although tribal governments are an American form of government by virtue of the Indian Reorganization Act of 1934 (IRA), tribal, state, and federal relations are unique because they are based on a relationship between two cultures that have biases toward each other. As is the case with most bias and prejudice, the intensity and consistency changes from person to person and region to region. As states and tribes differ, cultural biases are not the same from place to place.

State-tribal relations today vary. Some states have formal policies devised to work with Indian nations within a government-to-government framework, such as the states of Arizona and Utah. Other states, such as Alaska, still prefer to settle intergovernmental matters related to Indian tribes through the judicial system. Since the tribes and states recognize the cost of litigation, many have instituted alternative forms of intergovernmental dispute resolutions. These include intergovernmental agreements, sovereignty accords, and the development of policy procedures in tribal-state interaction.

Despite the legal framework for tribal and state government relations, the greatest barrier to a reciprocal relationship between tribal, state, and federal government is the perception that Indian reserves are regulatory voids and that tribal governing systems defy understanding. This is an attitude based not only on inaccurate information and understanding of the status of Indian reserves, but also a general ignorance about Indian-U.S. history and a narrow vision of the relationship between the tribes and states. The idea that Indian reserves are a regulatory void has also been enhanced by the shifting policies of the courts and Congress. If these federal institutions cannot come to terms with one another and cannot maintain any semblance of continuity in their own rulings and policies, how are the states and tribes to respond to one another?

Terry Williams, former director of the Environmental Protection Agency's American Indian Environmental Office, says, "The states in particular act as if there is a great Black Hole in Indian country. Instead of stepping over the threshold and digging in, they retreat inside their offices and do nothing. They should at least try and call Indian tribes; tribes do answer their telephones." However, with no clear guidance from the federal level, states may feel that any such attempts might prove futile. Any efforts at collaboration might be undermined through future policy shifts by Congress or the courts. With resources being in short supply, why waste the valuable time, energy, and money?

In the next six chapters we will discover that some states and tribes have been able to forge positive working relations despite the complexities created by the federal government. In the next several chapters we will look at individual cases in order to discover how cooperation can emerge within such a complex setting and what obstacles are yet to be overcome.

NOTES

1. Price, *Law and the American Indian*, p. 183.
2. *Native American Church v. Navajo Tribal Council*, 272 F2d 131 (1959).
3. Canby, *American Indian Law*.
4. Wilkins, *American Indian Politics*, p. 111.
5. Ibid.

6. Getches, Wilkinson, and Williams, *Federal Indian Law*, p. 193.
7. Lloyd Burton, *American Indian Water Rights and the Limits of the Law* (Lawrence, KS: University Press of Kansas, 1991).
8. *San Carlos Apache Tribe v. Arizona*, 463 U.S. 545 (1983).
9. *Colorado River Conservation District v. United States*, 424 U.S. at 820 (1976).
10. Public Law 280 (83-280, 67 Stat. 588).
11. Goldberg, *Public Law 280*, p. 543.
12. *Washington Review Code*, 37.12.010 (1976).
13. O'Brien, *Tribal Governments*.
14. Getches, Wilkinson, and Williams, Jr., *Federal Indian Law*, p. 482.
15. Retro cession was made a state option under a section of the 1968 Civil Rights Act. 25 U.S.C.A. at 1323.
16. *Seminole Tribe v. Florida*, 517 US 44 (1996).
17. Wilkins, *American Indian Politics*, p. 166.
18. Harris, Sachs, and Morris, "Honoring the Circle."
19. Wilkins, *American Indian Politics*, pp. 170–72.
20. *United States v. McBratney*, 104 US 621 (1881).
21. *Williams v. Lee*, 358 US 217 (1959).
22. *Organized Village of Kake v. Egan*, 369 US 60 (1962).
23. *Warren Trading Post v. Arizona Tax Commission*, 380 US 685 (1965).
24. *McClanahan v. Arizona State Tax Commission*, 411 U.S. 164, 93 S.Ct. 1257, 36 L.Ed. 2d 129 (1973).
25. Ibid.
26. *White Mountain Apache Tribe v. Bracker*, 448 US 136 (1980).
27. See Commission on State-Tribal Relations, *Handbook on State-Tribal Relations* (Albuquerque, NM: American Indian Law Center, n.d.) and Commission on State-Tribal Relations, *State-Tribal Agreements: A Comprehensive Study* (Albuquerque, NM: American Indian Law Center, 1981).
28. W. Dale Mason, "Tribes and States: A New Era in Intergovernmental Affairs," *Publius: The Journal of Federalism* 28, no. 1 (1998), pp. 111–30.
29. Ashley and Jarratt-Ziemski, "Superficiality and Bias."
30. Mason, "Tribes and States."
31. *Puyallup Tribe v. Washington Gaming Department*, 433 US 165 (1977).
32. *People v. Frank*, 101 CA, App. 3d, Supp 8 (1979).
33. *Donahue v. Justice Court*, 15 CA, App. 3d 557 (1971).
34. *Idaho et al. v. Coeur d'Alene Tribe of Idaho et al.*, 94 US 1474 (1997).
35. *Canadian St. Regis Band of Mohawk Indians v. New York*, 2nd District Court (2001).
36. *Navajo Nation v. United States*, AZ, U.S. Court of Appeals Ninth Circuit (1982).

PART II
Real World Tribal-State Interaction

CHAPTER 4

The Campo Band of Kumeyaay Indians

The Campo Indian Reservation is home to one band of the Kumeyaay Nation—the Campo Band of Kumeyaay Indians (also referred to as the Campo Band of Mission Indians and the Campo Band of Dieguenos Indians). While the Campo Reservation is comprised of about 17,000 acres, the area covered by the Kumeyaay Nation as a whole is much broader—extending from San Diego and Imperial Counties in southern California to some distance south of the Mexican border. The Kumeyaay have been a presence in the California coastal region since well before any European presence. In fact, the Quechan, the ancestors of the Kumeyaay, were well established when first encountered by the Spanish explorer Alarcon in 1540.[1] The first permanent European settlement in Kumeyaay territory was established in 1768.

Relations with the U.S. government and the territory of California were never warm, but the Kumeyaay and these other political entities managed to coexist. Then gold was discovered in northern California in 1848, and the first wave of 49ers began arriving one year later. Tensions began to rise and the federal government erected Fort Yuma in 1850 to secure the overland route into California.[2] The flood of Americans through the overland route drove the Kumeyaay from their territory and did nothing to foster positive relations between the original inhabitants and those who were new to the area.

An indication of the history of state-tribal relations can be found from the time that California became a state in 1850. One of the new state's first pieces of legislation was the "Act for the Government and Protection of Indians." This Act offered a direct challenge to *Worcester*, which recognized the Federal Government as the authority for dealing with Indians, by proclaiming that all regulation of Indians in California would occur at the state level. The Act also stripped native people of all rights normally extended to human beings. This early California law allowed for whites to take custody and control of Indian children; allowed for the arrest of unemployed Indians so that they could be hired out to whites; prohibited many traditional tribal customs, such as setting fire to grasslands for the management of the environment; and even made testimony by Indians inadmissible in cases against whites.[3]

Between 1851 and 1853, a series of treaties were negotiated with the various Indian tribes of California, but political pressure resulted in none of them being ratified by the state. Statewide sentiment toward Indians was clearly antagonistic. According to a recent document on Kumeyaay history,

The exploitation of Indian people in the areas of Mexican control, before the Mexican-American War, was criticized by visitors from the United States as cruel and inhuman. It was seen as providing a moral basis for the incorporation of California into the United States. After the war, criticism of the system was muted as the Americans expanded and transformed the system far beyond anything envisioned by the Mexicans.[4]

The hostilities toward Indians increased, and reports of murder, stolen land and property, and forced servitude mounted. Tribes were being decimated, and local governments were even known to pay bounties on heads or scalps of Indians. The result was a rapid decline in Indian populations in California. In 1845 the Indian population of California is estimated to have been 150,000. By 1855, the population had dropped to 50,000. For the Mountain Kumeyaay, a population of 2,000 in 1850 had dropped to 200 by 1890, a 90 percent loss.[5]

Finally, Congress passed "An Act for the Relief of the Mission Indians in the State of California" in 1891. It was through this Act and a subsequent executive order that the Campo Indian Reservation was created. The original reservation, created on February 10, 1893, was about one square mile (710 acres) near the town of Milguatay (Campo). While it was a step toward protecting what remained of the Kumeyaay, the one square mile of Campo was woefully inadequate for the population. The original one mile is referred to as "Old Campo" and is contained within the current Campo Band of Kumeyaay Indian Reservation, which is located in the eastern part of San Diego County in Southern California. The reservation consists of two detached land areas that cover a total area of 15,480 acres (24.2 square miles), located approximately 45 miles inland from the Pacific Ocean and 60 miles east of San Diego. All land on the Campo Indian Reservation is under trust status established under the Act of 1891 and is recognized by the Secretary of the Interior as a sovereign tribal government.

The Campo Band is governed by a General Council that consists of seven tribal council members and a tribal chairman who acts as the chief elected official (CEO). The form of tribal government is defined and established under the Campo Constitution, which was approved by the General Council in 1976. The General Council, as a self-governing political entity with internal sovereign powers, acts on all matters that pertain to the tribe, such as the tribal constitution, plans and policies, expenditures of annual tribal funds, proposed projects, individual use of tribal lands, and all other matters that are important to the tribe.[6]

The population of the Campo Band, according to the most recent figures, consists of about 250 people—the total reservation population, including non-Indians, is about 350.[7] Because of limited on-reservation opportunities, many tribal members work off the reservation in nearby San Diego.

Decades of abuse and neglect have degraded the ecosystem of the reservation. However, with assistance from the Indian Environmental General Assistance Program (GAP) of the EPA, the Campo Band established the Campo Environmental Protection Agency (CEPA) in 1990 to administer the band's regulatory infrastructure. Environmental protection on the reservation is delegated to the CEPA, which is touted by the EPA as one of its success stories.[8] The agency's primary goal is to provide a regulatory infrastructure to protect the environment and the health, safety, and welfare of reservation occupants and the surrounding communities by regulating environmental and public health resources on the reservation.[9] The CEPA operates under the oversight of a board of commissioners that consists of three members of the Campo Indian Tribe. The commissioners are appointed by the Chairman of the Campo Band with the advice and consent of the General Tribal Council.[10]

While the internal governance structure allows for the control of several programs and the creation of several tribal agencies—such as the CEPA—there is no tribal police department. California, as one of the original mandatory PL 280 states, has complete criminal jurisdiction over all persons residing on the Campo Reservation. There have been no moves for retrocession, and all police matters on the reservation are handled by the San Diego County Sheriff's Department.

STATE-TRIBAL RELATIONS

Environmental Management

Air Quality Management

California Assembly Bill-240 Chapter 805, Statutes of 1991 was signed by the governor of California in October 1991. This bill was enacted so that any Indian tribe in the state of California can enter into agreements with the state for purposes of cooperation in the implementation of environmental protection programs. Unfortunately for tribes within the state, the spirit of this law has never fully materialized. This is because of jurisdictional questions on the part of both the state and the tribes, and because the EPA has stepped up its efforts to work one-to-one with tribal governments. In fact, when asked if we could anticipate a formal agreement emerging between the Campo Tribe and the state of California, the manager of the tribal air quality program responded, "I don't think so. They are state, and we are federal. They are funded by the state and we are funded by the federal government."[11] In this sense, the efforts of the EPA are a double-edged sword when it comes to state-tribal relations. The grants offered by the EPA allow tribes to develop their own environmental programs (which is necessary for any cooperation to occur), but almost all the work is done at a federal-tribal level with very little state involvement (which can later add to the perception that states and tribes are inherently different and should not join forces because of jurisdictional concerns).

The Campo Department of the Environment has had an operational air quality program in place since 2000. As is the case with many tribes, the program came about through joint efforts with the EPA. By utilizing grant programs offered by the EPA, the tribe has been able to set its own regulations and develop testing and enforcement mechanisms to ensure that the requirements are being met. These efforts are not done in conjunction with the state of California. There have, however, been some efforts to work jointly in the area of air quality management. While the state is generally unwilling to devote resources to tribal matters that are outside their jurisdiction (and they have been slow to assert jurisdiction in this area as of late), the California Air Quality Board has informed the Campo Tribe that the board would be willing to take samples and provide the analysis if the tribe wanted them to do so. Such an offer is crucial in attempts to share resources and take a more cooperative approach to air quality management.[12]

Despite such efforts, the politics involved hinder greater cooperation—state taxpayers want money going to state programs. Also there is a city/mountain dynamic. The cities pollute more than the mountain areas in which the Campo Reservation is located. While tribal air has suffered from the smog emitted by the cities—primarily San Diego—the Campo do not have jurisdiction over non-tribal areas. They can regulate within their bounds but cannot enforce their regulations or standards on areas off the reservation—even if those areas are the principle cause of current problems. Attempts to do so are generally met with the charge that such requests are beyond the scope of tribal jurisdiction. Conversely, the state has attempted to regulate within tribal borders only to be told that it is outside of *its* jurisdiction. In this case, despite the fact that air doesn't respect borders, jurisdiction and politics are the primary obstacles to jointly managing air quality.

Water Quality Management

As with air quality, the Campo Environmental Protection Agency has developed a set of water quality standards in cooperation with the EPA. While the standards are currently under review, it is likely that they will be approved in 2003. While the state will have an opportunity to comment on the standards, chances are that they will raise no objections, since the tribal standards mirror those set by the state. As far as sharing resources and entering into cooperative agreements for the joint management of water resources, this is not something we are likely to see. In the words of Mike Connolly, head of the Campo EPA, "We don't really have joint management . . . there are a lot of things that go into the state-tribal relationship and it boils down to sovereignty. The tribes do not want to give up their sovereignty because their whole existence is based on sovereignty."[13]

It seems that with the Campo, as with many other tribes, whenever the state tries to encroach on the regulatory authority of the tribe, it becomes an issue of contention, and usually there are a lot of other forces that come into play that are hostile to Indian communities. In other words, politics has as much to do with the failure to cooperate as anything. Often, even if the state agency or agency member wants to have a cooperative relationship with the tribes, they may be forced into confrontation. This may be especially true in California, where the driving legislation is the California Environmental Quality Act—a process law that does not recognize tribal jurisdiction or land use planning and treats tribal communities just like any other community within the state. When the tribe attempts to assert its sovereign rights, it is frequently lambasted by environmental groups—employing the California law like a sledgehammer—for hiding behind sovereignty at the expense of the environment.

Part of the problem for the environment and efforts to jointly manage resources is that laws developed during the 1970s—when there was genuine environmental concern—can also be used as de facto zoning laws to stop development. If a group wants to restrict activities outside its jurisdiction, such as on a reservation, the group can attempt to use environmental laws as a tool to force tribes to comply with whatever plans are being made for use of adjacent lands. When looking at water quality management and other environmental areas, it boils down to environmental economics, and any negotiations start with an uneven playing field. San Diego and other municipalities have established sources of revenue and already have residential zones, downtown areas, and industrial zones. The tribe feels that now that the municipalities' remaining watershed sits on tribal land, suddenly the municipalities (and thus the state) are eager to protect these resources. In order to accomplish this, the cities want to limit the types of development in which tribes can engage by using environmental laws. The tribes' resentment comes from the fact that cities are attempting to protect resources they have destroyed themselves. The tribe suffers from polluted air and water—polluted by the cities, but cities don't share the revenue that came from the development. Moreover, on-reservation taxes for non-members are siphoned off and go to the state despite the fact that the tribe provides governmental services for them. According to Mike Connolly, "We want to protect the environment, but we are starting from an unequal position."[14] In other words, economics is another big concern when examining the state-tribal relationship, and the goals of the state and the tribe might not always be the same.

This is not to suggest that the state and tribe cannot reach an agreement over water-related issues. Depending on the people involved, and the ability to move beyond politics, there is hope. While those who work for governmental agencies are people who carry cultural biases with them, Connolly has noted that, by and large, the more professional the person, the better able they are to focus on the particular issue that is being confronted. If it is water quality, they are for higher standards. Those whose professionalism guides their decision-making are more able to take sovereignty as a given and work toward common solutions to pressing environmental problems. If there is an ulterior motive, then there is usually some kind of conflict. Unfortunately, according to Connolly, "We usually end up in conflict because most of the agencies and boards are under political control—at the staff level we may have good relations but at the board level it may be very hostile."[15]

Law Enforcement

As California is a PL 280 state, law enforcement falls outside of tribal jurisdiction, and there have been no attempts at obtaining retrocession. Therefore there are no real tribal-state cooperative efforts in this regard—all law enforcement falls to the San Diego Sheriff's Department. There are some problems with this situation, and tensions could spill over into other areas. For example, if the tribe feels that the sheriff does not respond to calls in a timely manner, this could be perceived as a sign of apathy on behalf of the county or state. Such a perception would undoubtedly hamper efforts to cultivate trust and foster cooperative efforts between the tribe and other state agencies.

Unfortunately, perception becomes reality in the case of law enforcement on the reservation. Many officers suffer from the misconception that the tribe is more accepting of crime than are whites in surrounding communities. Charges are often dropped or simply go unreported. To the officer who responds to the call only to have the charges dropped, this is a waste of time. They would rather devote their energy to obtaining convictions. What they do not realize is that the tribe, in many cases, operates under a different social structure and tends to handle many things internally through social mechanisms. This is not uniquely tribal—it is common to many tight-knit rural communities across the country, from tribes to Amish communities to isolated pockets of Appalachian whites. The result, however, is that outside law enforcement officials feel that their efforts are in vain. Of course, not all officers share this view, but the perception of some tribal members is that Campo calls are not given the same urgency as calls to other areas of the county. This perception is underscored by the funding for the department. The tribe does not pay for the sheriff's department—the county does. With scant resources, many feel that the attention goes to those areas that are more heavily populated and contribute more in tax dollars. Again, these are only perceptions—there are also those who feel that the San Diego Sheriff's Department devotes equal time to all areas of the county and that the reservation does not receive short shrift. According to tribal member Gilbert Pablo, "they respond when you call them."[16] For those who differ in their perception, however, other dealings with the state or county could be impacted without them even realizing it.

Other Issues

Casino

Tensions have risen between the Campo Tribe and San Diego County over the construction of a casino located on the highway between Tucson, Arizona, and San Diego, California. As always, there are many components to the conflict—politics and anti-gaming forces, tribal sovereignty, state involvement, and money.

The Campo Tribe signed a letter of agreement with a gaming corporation to finance a gambling facility on the reservation. The tribe was seeking to improve its economic condition through tapping into the traffic that passes by their reservation everyday. In order to move the project forward, the tribe had prepared an environmental impact statement (EIS) in 1999 in order to address any potential environmental concerns. At the time, the tribe was planning a rather small-scale operation in conjunction with a truck stop and restaurant. The 6,000-square-foot casino was planned as the last part of a four-stage development on the proposed site.

After the tribe compacted with the state, however, they decided to expand the size of the casino. Instead of 6,000 square feet, the new casino was to be closer to 60,000 square feet and was the main part of the development plan. Instead of being a fourth stage afterthought, the casino had become the priority. This did not sit well with several casino opponents in San Diego.

San Diego County officials asked the Bureau of Indian Affairs to intervene and halt construction of the project. The BIA refused to do so and stated that they could not intervene even if they wanted to. According to the BIA, the federal legislation clearly places any negotiations in the hands of the state and the tribe. In this case, the state and tribe had already negotiated a compact and the state, like the BIA, refused to intervene on behalf of the county. Instead, the state encouraged the tribe and the county to "meet and confer and work this out."[17]

Rather than meet face-to-face, however, the issue was played out in the press for quite some, time with county officials saying their calls were going unanswered and tribal officials saying they had no problems with the county and that the tribe would be happy to meet with them if they would come up to Campo. At one point, project coordinator Monique LaChappa stated, "If they would like to come up to Campo and visit our site, we'd be more than happy to have them."[18]

In this case, the conflict was more localized and occurred between the tribe and the county. There was apparently miscommunication, but neither side was meeting the other face-to-face to resolve the problem. To their credit, the state and federal government chose not to take sides and cloud the issue further. The same cannot be said with regard to a proposed landfill.

Landfill

Currently, there is an intergovernmental agreement between the Campo EPA and the California EPA. This agreement was specifically devised for a solid-waste recycling and disposal facility on the reservation. The Campo EPA regulations conform to the California Health and Safety Code and are functionally equal to state regulations. This conformity, no doubt, facilitated the intergovernmental agreement. The Campo EPA thus operates as a local enforcement agency that has adopted and approved a set of air quality regulations that will monitor the landfill operation under construction. With this understanding, the California EPA neither approved the Campo EPA air regulations, nor does the state exercise any authority in the jurisdiction of the Campo EPA.

During the development of the Tribal Implementation Plan, the Campo EPA felt that the state EPA personnel and local governments were more receptive and understanding after meetings held on a one-to-one basis with technical personnel. This mutual respect exists because the Campo EPA has highly qualified technical personnel who interact with the state personnel on an equal basis. The Campo EPA views state and local government environmental control staff as technical experts. Although this understanding exists, the state still posed obstacles.

Problems with the state arose because the Campo EPA was viewed as a competitor in the area of solid waste management. While San Diego County was initially receptive to the Campo proposal, their position quickly changed when they were told that the landfill would be tribally run and that proceeds would stay with the tribe (the county had assumed that they would simply lease the facility from the tribe). County officials quickly turned the heads of several key state policy-makers. Some California state policy-makers adopted misconceptions that were being advanced by San Diego County. These policy-makers viewed the Campo EPA as incapable of monitoring and operating environmental programs. It was felt that a stereotypical image of Indian reservations (as poor or incompetent enforcers) and a homogenized view of Indian tribes and culture (e.g., tribes all have the same opinions and priorities) tend to permeate the perceptions of state policy-makers. Clearly such stereotypes have to be addressed in order to improve state-tribal relations.

Despite problems with the state, several predominant factors made the intergovernmental agreement between the Campo EPA and the California EPA a success. First, to address the fear of unsafe and/or substandard tribal regulatory enforcement, CEPA not only conforms to the California standards, but also allows state environmental officials to have access to the site of the landfill and information relevant to the project. CEPA then would have access to the state's technical assistance. Jurisdictional issues are precluded since the landfill regulatory standards are as strict as the state air quality standards.[19]

The California EPA and CEPA also agreed that state agencies would assist in providing services such as facility inspection, permit preparation, enforcement of solid wastes that are collected, standards, and compliance hearings. CEPA would then pay state agencies for the services provided. Clearly, the agreement works because Campo dispelled the common perceptions held by local and state governments that Indian reservations are havens for pollution and that the reservation environment is unregulated or poorly regulated.

Despite the agreement, numerous interest groups filed suit to halt the construction of the landfill, and one member of the California Assembly attempted to pass a bill that would strip the tribe of jurisdiction. The bill was unsuccessful (it would have been thrown out anyway as an illegal intrusion into tribal sovereignty), and the tribe finally prevailed in court. As of 2002, the landfill is moving forward as planned despite many state- and county-led attempts to derail the project.

Naval Training Center Land

When the United States began closing military bases, an interesting question arose—what should be done with the land? Many tribes sought to acquire the rights to the land since the federal government had done such a historically poor job of preserving land allotments designated through treaties. In Arizona the Gila River Indian Tribe was able to obtain a golf course and 10 percent stake in any development of the Williams Air Force Base. In Washington the Muckleshoot Tribe reached an agreement to acquire most of the Sand Point Naval Base after it closed.[20] In an attempt to follow suit, the Campo Tribe petitioned the Department of Defense for direct transfer of the land being opened up by the closing of a naval training center in San Diego. Since this was ancestral land, the tribe felt that they had a good case. The Department of Defense disagreed and granted decision-making power to the San Diego City Council. Not surprisingly, the council came up with a development plan that would benefit the city and private developer Corky McMillin Cos.—a plan that the military approved.

In order to stop the transfer, the Campo Tribe was forced to join forces with other bands of Kumeyaay and file a federal lawsuit. In the words of one lawsuit consortium member, "We're coastal Indians, but we have no coast."[21] Round one of the potentially long-term and costly battle went to the tribe when a federal judge in Washington, D.C., issued a temporary order halting the transfer of land from the military to the city.[22]

With millions of dollars riding on this issue, the tribe and city are in direct conflict. This underpins the economic concerns raised by Mike Connolly when discussing water quality and the conflict with surrounding areas. This is not so much a lack of cooperation between the state and tribe, but more of what appears to be an ongoing struggle between the Campo Tribe and San Diego County. State-tribal relations will be strengthened, or hampered, to the extent to which the county is successful in getting the state to side with it and offer support in its struggles with the tribe.

SUMMARY AND KEY POINTS

In the case of the Campo Tribe and California, there does not appear to be a tremendous amount of cooperation. That said, there also does not appear to be much in the way of outright conflict either. In the areas of air and water quality management, the tribe is working directly with the EPA and is receiving funding from the federal government to establish and enforce its own standards. The tribe and state seem to be comfortable with separate sources of funding for separate jurisdictions. There are occasional cases where the state will intervene on behalf of San Diego County and try to assert jurisdiction, but the state is generally rebuffed by the tribe. There are no plans for sharing of information or resources between the state and tribe, and formal cooperative agreements are not likely. There are informal contacts among the technical people and relations at that level remain positive and cordial.

The main source of conflict between the state and tribe emerges from county-tribal conflict. In the case of the proposed landfill, the state and tribe had actually signed a cooperative agreement before the county got involved and rallied state support in opposition to the project. This state-tribal agreement was facilitated through face-to-face communication and the recognition on both sides that the state and tribe were both technically proficient and that both sides shared similar goals in this particular area. It was only when things moved beyond the technical realm and into the political realm that things began to fall apart.

From this case it seems that the following are crucial for forging cooperative agreements:

1. Face-to-face communication—the state and tribe were able to accomplish this and an agreement was signed. The tribe and county tended to talk about each other rather than to each other when it came to the casino issue, and relations became even more strained.
2. Focus on a single issue—there are always going to be ongoing discussions and disagreements. If these are allowed to enter into a discussion, negotiation is doomed. The state and tribe were able to forge a cooperative agreement by separating out the single issue of landfill standards from other issues such as land claims, gaming, and the like.
3. Recognize sovereignty—to the tribe this is the source of their very existence. To ignore sovereignty is to end any hope for cooperation. On a similar note, the tribe needs to recognize that the state is a sovereign entity that has its own set of goals. Cooperation will only emerge when the goals of both sides are taken into account. In the case of the landfill agreement, the tribe maintained jurisdiction over the management of the landfill. State integrity and sovereignty was respected by the tribe mirroring the standards laid down by the state and by acknowledging that the state had much to offer in the way of technical assistance and information.
4. Avoid politics—of course this is impossible, since both sides are inherently political and must respond to their respective constituents. However, it is clear that those working closest to an issue—the technocrats—are more concerned with the issue at hand than the broader political implications. Water quality experts on both sides simply want clean water. This explains why lower-level employees of the California EPA have offered to provide sampling and testing assistance but such gestures have not led to broader cooperation or formal agreements. When negotiations move higher up the chain of command, the players are inherently more concerned with the politics and the issue itself can become obscured.
5. Look to other levels of government—in the case of the Campo Band of Kumeyaay and the state of California, San Diego County cannot be ignored. The bulk of the external tension facing the tribe is coming from the county. More-

over, there have been instances where the county has drawn the state into the battle that has hampered state-tribal relations. As cities and counties are the closest in proximity to reservation land, it is inevilabelle that these governments enter into the mix. The extent to which both states and tribes are able to handle dealings with these third parties will undoubtedly be a factor in state-tribal negotiations and cooperative efforts.

NOTES

1. http://www.campo-kumeyaay.org/history.htm.
2. Ibid.
3. Ibid.
4. Ibid.
5. Ibid.
6. *Campo Indian Reservation Nonpoint Assessment Report*, June 1993.
7. U.S. Department of Commerce, *American Indian Reservation and Indian Trust Areas* (Washington, D.C.: U.S. Government Printing Office, 1996).
8. U.S. Environmental Protection Agency, Region 9, "Campo Band of Kumeyaay Indians' Environmental Success Story," *Indian Program News*, October 1998.
9. *Campo Indian Reservation Tribal Water Quality Assessment Report*, November 1994.
10. *Campo Band of Mission Indians Environmental Policy Act of 1990 as Amended*, December 1994.
11. Gilbert Pablo, interview by Jeff Ashley, telephone interview, July 2002, on file with author.
12. Ibid.
13. Mike Connolly, interview by Jeff Ashley, telephone interview, July 2002, on file with author.
14. Ibid.
15. Ibid.
16. Pablo, interview.
17. John Castaldo, "Campo Casino Has County Upset: Project 10 Times as Big as Before," *San Diego Union-Tribune*, 10 May 2001.
18. Ibid.
19. *Cooperative Agreement between the Campo Environmental Protection Agency and the State of California*, 10 December 1992.
20. Bart Jansen, "Tribes Turn to Former Military Bases," AP Online, 20 January 2000.
21. Ibid.
22. Ronald Powell, "U.S. Halts Shift of NTC Land to City: Ancestral-home Suit by Tribes to Be Heard First," *San Diego Union-Tribune*, 12 May 2000.

CHAPTER 5

The Navajo Nation

The Navajo people call themselves *Dineh*, or "The People." They were originally from the North, but migrated to the Southwest during the 1400s and were first encountered by outsiders sometime between the 1400s and 1500s in the area surrounding the San Juan River. The first outsiders to encounter the Dineh were the Spaniards, who brought with them horses, which were quickly adopted into the traditional nomadic lifestyle of the Navajo.[1]

The four clans (there are now over sixty) hunted and gathered, occasionally raiding nearby Hopi villages for supplies. However, as time passed, the Navajo people began to settle down into a less transient way of life. Rather than continuing to move about, the integration of farming allowed them to remain largely in one area. Many began to weave, make pottery, farm, and raise herds of sheep and goats while living in permanent homes (hogans).[2]

From the time of the first meeting with the Spaniards, the Navajo were able to basically go about their daily affairs without major disruption. There were skirmishes, and during the 1800s the conflict between the Navajo and some Mexican settlers became quite severe at times. There were, however, no actual wars between the two parties. War would not occur until the creation of the United States and intrusion by that new nation into Indian country.[3]

The rise in conflict between the United States and the Navajo people led to the first treaty between these two nations in 1846. Unfortunately, there were continuing disagreements over treaty compliance. Among these breakdowns was the failure on the part of the United States to recognize the importance of clans and differences between tribal members—not everyone had agreed to the terms of the treaty. Despite the fact that these distinct tribal units often made differing decisions, and not all were consulted in the treaty negotiations, the army held *all* Navajo responsible for all treaty promises.[4] This led to problems and the perception of treaty violations on the part of the U.S. government, which subsequently sent in troops to resolve the problem. The troops were instructed to do whatever was necessary to secure the land and restore order. In the words of historian Duane Champagne, "The United States was willing to adopt extreme military measures to subdue the Indians and control their land base."[5] Under the direction of trader turned army colonel Kit Carson, land was torched, sheep slaughtered, and livelihood destroyed until the people faced starvation and finally gave in to the U.S. government in 1863–64. It was then that the Navajo people were forced by Carson and the army to take the Long Walk[6]

Some 8,000 Navajo were rounded up and forced to walk from their homeland in the high desert of Northern Arizona to Fort Sumner in a desolate portion of what is now eastern New Mexico. Along the way, many people died. Once at the military camp in the barren Bosque Redondo region, the Navajo people suffered. Battles with other tribes, lack of food, crop failures, and disease all took their toll. By the time a new treaty was signed in 1868, close to one quarter of the Navajo at Fort Sumner had died.[7]

The treaty signed in 1868 allowed the Navajo to return home and established the Navajo Reservation. Additional land was added to the reservation in 1884 and again in the 1900s. In addition to the grants, the tribe has been successful in making several land purchases to increase the physical size of the Navajo Nation considerably. Today, the Navajo Indian Reservation located in northern Arizona, northwestern New Mexico, and southern Utah covers 25,516 square miles (16,193,358 acres), which is approximately the size of the state of West Virginia. The Navajo Nation is geographically the largest Indian nation in the United States and with approximately 219,097 people it has one of the largest populations.[8] The Arizona portion of the reservation covers Apache, Navajo, and Coconino Counties. San Juan and McKinley Counties make up the New Mexico portion, with San Juan County covering the Utah reservation. Additionally, the land base of the New Mexico portion of the reservation is checkerboarded and lies east of the principal reservation. These lands cover about four thousand square miles. Parts of the land are held in trust, while others are fee lands and allotments. Other sections include tribal-owned land, Bureau of Land Management (BLM) land, state lands, national park land areas, federal ownership of minerals found in land areas, and finally land owned by the railroad. There are also the satellite reservations. These are the communities of Alamo, Canoncito, and Ramah. They are tracts of land that are all in New Mexico and are detached from the main reservation on the New Mexico portion. The Hopi Indian Reservation is within the southwestern part of the Navajo Reservation covering 2.4 million acres. The reservation boundaries are also contiguous to several city governments. These "bordertowns" include Flagstaff, Page, Winslow, and Holbrook, Arizona; and Farmington, Grants, and Gallup, New Mexico. Gallup is within the exterior boundaries of the reservation.

The Navajo Tribe fought against the Indian Reorganization Act and was granted the opportunity to hold their own constitutional convention. The Navajo Tribe came up with a plan for a government that would operate completely separate from the Office of Indian Affairs (later the BIA). This was rejected by the Secretary of the Interior (the Department of the Interior housed the Office of Indian Affairs). While the Navajo plan would have meant greater independence and political freedom, this was not to be at that time. The Secretary of the Interior created a Navajo Business Council, which largely remains the center of the modern Navajo Nation.[9]

The political and legal structure of the Navajo tribal government consists of judicial, executive, and legislative bodies in a three-branch government. The Navajo Tribal Council (legislature) is the official governing body. Tribal elections are held every four years to elect the president, vice-president, and 88 members of the tribal council delegates. These councilmen represent the 110 chapters. Chapter Houses are local political units where one may discuss local community concerns and political, social, and economic issues.

The tribal council is divided into various subcommittees such as the Advisory Committee, the Budget and Finance Committee, the Health and Social Services Committee, and the Intergovernmental Relations Committee. In 1989, the Navajo Nation amended Title II to the Navajo Tribal Code (NTC). The NTC is divided into 24 titles that deal with all functions of the tribal governing system. Therefore, Title II defines the power relationships among the tribal council, the executive, and the judicial functions of the tribe. Consequently, the tribal chairman and vice-chairman are now president and vice-president of the tribal council. The legislative branch now also has a speaker of the Navajo Nation Tribal Council.[10]

STATE-TRIBAL RELATIONS

> The key is commitment of resources and commitment to carrying out the basic mission of whatever it is that you set out to do—whether this is protecting the air, water, or community from crime.
> – Francis Bradley, Navajo Police

Environmental Management

Air Quality Management

The Navajo Tribe has worked for, and received, treatment as a state by the EPA and has had its air quality standards approved. In addition to setting the standards, the Navajo Air Quality Control Program has regulatory and enforcement authority on the reservation. In the Navajo's attempts to maintain clean air for the Navajo Nation, the tribe is encountering similar attempts by the states of New Mexico, Arizona, and Utah. Since the vast majority of tribal lands are located in Arizona and New Mexico, we will focus on the relationship between the Navajo Nation and those two states. This case provides a great study in positive and negative relations, because while the tribe remains a constant in the two relationships, and its overall position does not change, levels of cooperation and coordination with the states differ.

The Navajo Nation Environmental Protection Agency's Air Quality Control Program (NAQCP) has worked well with the Arizona Department of Environmental Quality (ADEQ). Although intergovernmental relations among top tribal government and state officials vary with each issue, the air quality program has received technical assistance from the ADEQ. This is evident because the current tribal air code was not only developed with the assistance of ADEQ, but was also fashioned after the state's air quality regulations. In the past, the state and tribe have engaged in the sharing of information and have provided technical support and assistance to one another. This is due, in part, to the Navajo Tribal Council's Intergovernmental Relations Committee (IRC), established in 1983, and an ADEQ policy for dealing with tribal governments that was developed in 1994. The function of the IRC is to represent the interests of the Navajo Nation in its governmental relations with federal agencies, states, counties, municipalities, and other tribal governments.[11] With the Statement of Policy the Navajo Nation tribal divisions, departments, and agencies are allowed to enter into informal agreements, such as cooperative agreements, memoranda of understanding, and intergovernmental agreements. These agreements are based on mutual issues and problems, cooperation, coordination, and a mutual respect for the sovereignty of both the Navajo Nation and the state of Arizona. Department directors and technical personnel also have continuous dialogue and training on issues related specifically to air quality.

The ADEQ policy explicitly states that the agency recognizes the Navajo Nation as a government that has the sovereign right to hold exclusive jurisdiction over Indian country. The ADEQ goes on to add that historically the EPA has provided more funding to states than tribes and it is in the interest of the state to see that tribal capacity in enhanced. It is the state's position that they will provide any reasonable support requested by the tribe—the key is that the policy directs the agency to get involved only if asked and that any such assistance "will not be used as the basis for assertion of state authority within Indian country."[12]

For the most part, the state and tribe have lived up to the tenets of their respective policies and directives—sovereignty has been respected on both sides, and a certain level of professional cooperation has been exhibited. There was, however, a question about the jurisdiction of the Navajo Generating Station, the largest source of pollution for the reservation and also a major source of power for the state of Arizona. Since the state and tribe have air quality standards that mirror one another, there really should not have been too much of a problem. However, prior to the establishment of the tribal program and the application to be dealt with as a state, the generating station had been regulated by the ADEQ. After the program was developed, the ADEQ was not ready to simply hand over the regulation of the plant—despite the fact that it operates on the reservation. In this case, the EPA stepped in and assured the state that they and the tribe were capable of handling the plant. The combination of EPA pressure, the legal jurisdiction of the tribe, and the recently adopted ADEQ policy for dealing with tribes led to the transfer of authority to the tribe in the late 1990s.[13]

As of 2002, relations remain positive, but there are no plans for joint management, and the tribe is taking more of an independent position. While there is no animosity and the tribe would certainly cooperate if cooperation were in its interest, the adoption of the tribe-as-state status and support from the EPA have convinced the tribe that they can do things by themselves. When asked if there were plans for any state-tribal cooperative agreements or memorandums of understanding (MOUs), an official with the Navajo Air Quality Program responded, "We don't need to."[14] The New Mexico portion of the Navajo Reservation is checkerboarded. This has always caused problems in intergovernmental relations not only in environmental matters, but also in other programs. Unlike the cooperative efforts with Arizona that were needed to get the tribal program functioning, the checkerboarded nature of the reservation has affected relations. The checkerboarded area of the Navajo Reservation is partly held in trust; others are fee lands, BLM lands, tribally owned lands, and allotted lands. Other tracts include state lands, national park lands, and federal ownership of minerals found in this part of the reservation. Staff members indicate that current relations can be described as "average." Having multiple jurisdictional problems in New Mexico, a Statement of Policy was signed by the Navajo Tribal President in 1992 asking tribal divisions and departments to discuss and negotiate solutions to common problems with the state. The flexibility lies in the fact that all agreements are issue-driven and are intended to solve problems of mutual concern.[15] Despite the granting of authority to the department heads, no MOUs have been developed with the state of New Mexico and none are anticipated—the jurisdictional divide over non-trust land within the borders of the reservation is too great.

Water Quality Management

The Navajo Tribal Council approved a set of water quality standards for the Navajo EPA to follow, but the standards had not received final approval by the EPA as of 2002. Pending approval, which would grant the tribe primacy for water quality regulation and enforcement on the reservation, these responsibilities fall to the EPA and the federal government. Since the tribal standards essentially mirror those of the surrounding states, there should not be any state opposition. The one issue where tribal standards will differ is that of selenium levels. There is a naturally high level of selenium in the Four Corners region, and the tribe feels that selenium poses a threat to the health of its citizens. The states have not raised any concern over the higher standard, but several companies (particularly those engaged in mining) have pushed for more lax regulation from the tribe. They argue that since the higher levels of selenium occur naturally, regulations should not be even more strict. The extent to which these companies will obtain political support is yet to be seen, and the notice and comment period for the proposed tribal water standards is rapidly approaching as of 2002. The water quality standards are important because they reflect the different relationships between the tribe and surrounding governments. The tribe knows what to expect from Utah, Arizona, federal agencies, and various pueblos—they don't know what type of comments they will receive from New Mexico. Given the history of Navajo encounters with the state, the tribe doesn't feel very confident that New Mexico will recognize tribal authority.[16]

The relationship between the Navajo Nation and the state of Arizona concerning water management is very similar to that concerning air quality. Since the ADEQ passed the 1994 policy for dealing with tribal governments, there is a framework in place for respecting sovereign rights and for providing assistance whenever it is feasible and requested. There are several issue-specific MOUs between Arizona and the tribe that specify that the state will provide technical assistance and training—something that falls in line with the policy of helping to expand the capacity of tribal environmental programs.

Three primary factors have played into the successful negotiation of the Arizona-Navajo Nation MOUs for water: a focus on the issue, discussions that began with technical people, and clear jurisdiction. In focusing on the issue, both sides have recognized that streams are shared and travel through both jurisdictions. This has necessitated knowledge on each side about what the other is doing. Information sharing is an integral part of all the agreements. The second factor is that the discussions have begun at the technical level. While the ADEQ policy and tribal approval have allowed for the talks to begin, the specifics originated with technical people who tend to share similar goals. It is easier for these people to ignore the jurisdictional issues and focus on the best way to promote water quality. Once there is agreement at this level, and support on both sides, it is easier to obtain the signatures of higher level, more political administrators. The final, perhaps most critical factor (at least the one that distinguishes Arizona from New Mexico) is clarity over jurisdiction. The primary obstacle to negotiating MOUs and cooperation with New Mexico is jurisdiction. Most of the reservation's checkerboarding occurs in New Mexico and the checkerboarding creates confusion and tension. According to the head of the Navajo Water Program,

> We know that every time we sit down with New Mexico jurisdiction is going to be an issue. We feel we have jurisdiction, and they think they do. With Arizona, we know we have the jurisdiction—there is no issue to that.[17]

The result? Positive relations and numerous MOUs with Arizona and none with New Mexico. Until the jurisdictional issue is resolved, relations will remain tense between New Mexico and the tribe in a number of issue areas—not just environmental management.

Law Enforcement

The relationship between the Navajo Tribal Police and surrounding jurisdictions really points to the fact that the goals and attitudes of states, counties, and cities differ. The relationship between the tribe and New Mexico differs from its relationship with Arizona. Similarly, relationships differ between the tribe and various counties in Arizona. The one constant is the tribe.

The head of the Navajo Police Department has come up with a useful working definition of interagency cooperation. To him, cooperation is the sharing and commitment of resources. In this sense cooperation is more than passive agreement over an issue—it is consciously acting on the agreement and putting time, money, and resources behind a joint effort that is respectful of each side's cultural and political way of doing things. The Navajo Nation cooperates with Arizona. The relationship between the tribe and the state of Arizona is solid. In fact, all officers in Arizona are certified—including the Navajo Police. Certified peace officers can enforce the law anywhere in the state. The only limit is that tribal officers would be acting as Arizona officers and would be following Arizona's laws and procedures. The tribe has sent officers to help in areas such as Winslow, Holbrook, White River, and Flagstaff. In doing this, the tribe has committed its resources and has done so in a manner that respects and preserves the sovereignty of the state—they have gone as state officers, not tribal officers. The laws of the tribe and the procedures they generally follow on the reservation were set aside in favor of state laws and procedures.[18] Unlike Arizona, the state of New Mexico limits tribal jurisdiction. While the Navajo police officers are certified as peace officers in New Mexico, they are limited to reservation areas. While the tribe would probably provide assistance as they do in Arizona, they are not legally allowed to in New Mexico.

Just as state-tribal relations differ, there are varying degrees of cooperation between the Navajo Nation and surrounding counties. Several Arizona counties are seeking mutual aid agreements with the tribe. This differs from cross-deputization, which would require Navajo Nation laws to be enforced on tribal land and state/county laws being enforced outside. With cross-deputization, officers have the authority to act as one of their counterparts without the other being present. There has been some reluctance because of tort claims as a result of enforcing tribal laws. Also, this would mean using county resources to support tribal laws, courts, and the justice system, which may not be politically acceptable (Navajo County would actually be interested in cross-commissioning—Apache and Coconino Counties are not). Mutual aid agreements are a step below this and give authority to cooperating agencies in specific situations. In other words, unlike cross-deputization, which tends to focus on who can arrest whom, mutual aid agreements are about helping each other out in certain situations that occur on the reservation and in surrounding areas.

While the aid agreements would provide for the sharing of resources and more rapid response to crisis situations, there are some sticking points in the negotiations. The tribe is much more willing to negotiate and agree to a mutual aid situation (thus agreeing to commit tribal resources) with counties that have shown support for tribal efforts in the past and have given as much as they have received. When Apache County has 16 officers stationed near the reservation while both Navajo and Coconino Counties have only 1, there is a clear indication of mutual commitment.[19]

The main issue deals with adapting to tribal law when on the reservation. County agencies are willing to accept the resources of the tribe and are willing to offer some assistance, but they do not want to deal with the added bureaucratic burden of dealing with another government's set of rules. According to the Navajo official responsible for negotiating mutual aid agreements with surrounding counties, the main condition for reaching a compromise is a willingness to enforce the nation's laws within the existing structure that the nation has in place. According to him, "That is the nation's primary mission. If you come here, you will do what we do *the way we do it*—that becomes the sticking point for agencies who feel that process is too cumbersome."[20] In other words, the preservation of sovereignty is the key issue that is going to determine whether any of the mutual aid agreements actually go into effect and whether the tribe and county governments are going to enter into a cooperative venture.

Other Issues

Unlike many of the smaller tribes, the Navajo Nation is a formidable force. They have the land base, the numbers, and the resources to back up any proposal that they may have. They are able, more so than most, to maintain sovereign integrity. When the Navajo Tribe talks, people listen. When then-president Albert Hale proposed a one-day roadblock on the Navajo Reservation as a "lesson in sovereign rights," it was noticed. With 25,000 acres extending into three states and bisecting a portion of the major east-west corridor, I-40, such a move would have tied up traffic for miles. People would have understood sovereignty. Of course, such a move never took place, but the mere mention, by the largest tribe in the country, was news.[21] With its size and resources, the tribe can be a political force. One area of concern has to do with the dilution of political and civic voice.

Political/Civic Rights

While our analysis has focused on relations with Arizona and New Mexico, a civil rights lawsuit against the Utah Judicial Council and the Seventh District judges could provide a model to follow in other states. The Utah case stems from the fact that there were no American Indians on the San Juan County jury pool list from 1932 to 1970—despite the fact that Navajo and Ute tribal members constituted almost half of the county's population. While the lawsuit sparked a revision and the number of Indian jurors increased, the issue reminded tribal members that they are not always extended the full civil rights that they deserve.[22] Closer attention is now being paid to surrounding jurisdictions and there has been an erosion of trust—something that could hamper future relations.

Another area of concern—still dealing with representation and ability to function as equals within the political and legal system—is that of legislative redistricting. As we have seen, the relations between the tribe and the state of New Mexico are not stellar when it comes to law enforcement or environmental management. Now there is concern that the legislative districts in New Mexico have historically been gerrymandered in an attempt to dilute the voting power of the Navajo Nation. Relying on the testimony of a college professor from the University of New Orleans who stated that Navajo country legislative districts appear to have been "packed," the tribe offered the state an alternative plan for the recent redistricting—one that was ignored.[23] With the tribe making reference to the Voting Rights Act, one can only imagine that there is a potential lawsuit on the horizon—something that cannot better the already tense relations between the Navajo Nation and the state of New Mexico.

Arizona is being watched carefully as well. While most of the Navajo Nation residing in Arizona traditionally voted in the same district, initial redistricting plans had them being split into two. With no Navajo members on the Arizona redistricting commission (glaringly no minorities at all), there were bound to be some questions about what motivated the split.[24] Even if the district remains intact, there may be some question about whether the tribe has the support in Phoenix and the state legislature that they thought they did. The perception of mutual support is very important for maintaining the positive, cooperative relationship that Arizona and the Navajo Nation currently enjoy.

SUMMARY AND KEY POINTS

When examining the relationship and level of cooperation between the Navajo Nation and surrounding governments, it becomes apparent that the tribe works better and more closely with Arizona than it does with New Mexico. It also appears to work with Apache County in Arizona better than it does with other counties in the same state. From these differences we can pinpoint some of the factors that are contributing to the positive efforts in Arizona and isolate the primary obstacle to forming a similar relationship in New Mexico—namely the jurisdictional cloud created by the checkerboard of tribal and fee lands. The factors that seem to promote positive relations and are necessary in forming formal cooperative agreements such as MOUs include:

1. Allow the technical people to initiate discussion—for all of the MOUs with the state of Arizona, the initial discussion and framework was taken over by the people in the field who would be charged with implementing the agreement. These people knew what they needed and what they could offer. They were also able to agree on the nature of the problem without getting burdened with larger jurisdictional questions. For instance, they were able to agree that the streams were a shared resource—no small task when discussing western water. If the discussion had begun at higher levels, it is quite possible that jurisdictional obstacles would have overshadowed the problem at hand.

2. A guiding framework or policy is helpful—while it is useful to have talks begin at the technical level, the people at this level must receive both direction and flexibility in order to stimulate the talks. The lower-level technical people can feel secure and supported when they approach one another on an issue—the 1992 tribal statement of policy and the 1994 ADEQ policy for dealing with tribes clearly send the signal that cooperation is encouraged and supported. No such directive has been given to the environmental people in New Mexico, and relations between the state and tribe are merely cordial—not highly cooperative.

3. Cooperation is sharing resources and respecting mechanisms—this concept is particularly helpful when looking at the relationship between any agencies or governments. Is there a true commitment to solving a common problem, or is an entity merely paying lip service to an issue? Providing resources—giving and not just taking—will help to facilitate cooperative agreement. In the case of the ADEQ and the tribe, the ADEQ provided much-needed technical support when the tribe was initially establishing its own air quality program. In the case of the mutual aid agreement under discussion between the tribe and several Arizona counties, the tribe is much more willing to enter into a mutual agreement when they are convinced that it will, in fact, be mutual.

More than simply giving resources, however, the definition of cooperation provided by Francis Bradley includes respect for existing mechanisms designed to solve problems. Whether these mechanisms are state laws or tribal water quality standards, they must be respected. This is, of course, the recognition of sovereignty.

4. Work on resolving jurisdiction/the danger of checkerboarding—the Arizona portion of the Navajo Reservation is fairly intact, while the New Mexico portion is severely broken up. When both sides *know* who has jurisdiction, other topics can emerge—such is the case with Arizona. The ongoing jurisdictional disputes between the Navajo Nation and New Mexico are forcing both sides into a corner and neither one will make a move toward the middle. The result is that the tribe will not allow for any intrusion onto the reservation and New Mexico will not allow any tribal efforts off of trust property—even for officers who are state-certified. Until there is federal clarification on the jurisdiction in these mixed areas that covers *every* issue clearly and precisely, there is bound to be tension at the legislative, council, and higher administrative levels. It is possible that a crisis may emerge that leaves the two sides no alternative but to cooperate, but until then the jurisdictional uncertainty and turf wars will most likely continue to keep these two governments at odds.

NOTES

1. http://www.nps.gov/nava/nav.htm.
2. http://www.arizona.com/indians/navajo.html.
3. Ibid.
4. http://www.nps.gov/nava/nav.htm.
5. Duane Champagne, *Native America: Portrait of the Peoples* (Washington, D.C.: Visible Ink Press, 1994), p. 135.
6. Ibid. See also http://www.arizona.com/indians/navajo.html.
7. Ibid.
8. *Chapter Images: General Facts on the Navajo Chapters,* May 1990.
9. Champagne, *Native America,* pp. 135–36.
10. Albert Hale and Louis Denetsosi, *The Navajo Nation: Title II Amendments of 1989.*
11. Navajo Nation, Navajo Tribal Code, title 2, sec. 871, 1982.
12. Arizona Department of Environmental Quality, *ADEQ Tribal Government Policy,* no. 0003.001. Issued 4 February 1994 and amended 9 May 1997.
13. U.S. Environmental Protection Agency, "Source Specific Federal Implementation Plan for Navajo Generating Station," *Federal Register,* vol. 64, no. 173, 8 September 1999.
14. Tribal air official, interview by Jeff Ashley, telephone interview, August 2002, on file with author.
15. D. Kelly, interview by Secody Hubbard, personal interview, May 1995.
16. Patrick Antonio, interview by Jeff Ashley, telephone interview, April 2002, on file with author.
17. Ibid.
18. Francis Bradley, interview by Jeff Ashley, telephone interview, April 2002, on file with author.

19. Ibid.

20. Ibid.

21. Leslie Linthicum, "Tribes Consider Roadblocks," *Albuquerque Journal*, 29 January 1998.

22. "Utah County to Add Indians to Jury Rolls," *Albuquerque Journal*, 30 June 1996.

23. Richard Benke, "Navajo Tribe Wants Six Navajo-Majority House Districts," Associated Press State and Local Wire, 7 January 2002.

24. "Navajos Worry Redistricting Will Water Down Their Clout," Associated Press State and Local Wire, 2 July 2001.

CHAPTER 6

The Puyallup Tribe

The Puyallup Tribe descended from the tribes and bands located in villages on the Puyallup River, Commencement Bay, and Vashon Island (Homamish People). In 1854, the original Puyallup Reservation was established with the signing of the Treaty of Medicine Creek. This treaty set aside a mere 1,280 acres for the reservation. Executive orders in 1857 and 1873 increased the size of the Puyallup Reservation and the allotment of the reservation was finished in 1886. The current size of the reservation is 18,062 acres and includes portions of three Washington cities—Tacoma, Milton, and Fife.[1]

With land set aside, the tribe went about its business of fishing and growing crops such as wheat and oats in surrounding meadow areas. However, as with many other tribes, external pressure would begin to be placed on state and federal politicians to open up tribal reserves for occupancy and use by non-Indians. In the case of the Puyallup the pressure was coming primarily from the growing population of Tacoma. Rapid growth of this city caused citizens to seek removal of restrictions on allotted reservation lands. On August 19, 1890, Congress finally succumbed to the pressure and authorized the sale of Puyallup Reservation tracts. The proposed sale of tribal land became more of a reality on March 3, 1893, when further congressional action established a commission to select and appraise tracts for the upcoming sale. The only land exempt from the public sale were those tracts required for Indian homes and land necessary for maintaining a school—everything else was subject to selection by the commission. The 1893 statute allowed for the tribe to keep any land that was not sold, but placed restrictions on what the tribe could do with any land that they had remaining.[2] The tribe could not sell the land on their own for a period of ten years. After the ten years non-Indians could deal directly with the Indians. As a result of the public land sale and subsequent tribal land sales, the composition of land ownership and the make-up of residents on the reservation changed dramatically. Currently, the 18,062-acre reservation, located in Pierce County, is almost entirely held in fee status. Of the total acreage, only 103.26 acres are currently in tribal or trust hands. Of this relatively small amount, 30.28 acres are held in trust for the 1,800 enrolled Puyallup Tribe members.[3] The reservation population is about 32,500, of which only around 1,000 are Indians. The jurisdictional problems arising from this situation are apparent. Some jurisdictional issues, however, were settled by an agreement with the state.

The Puyallup Tribe realized that the widespread taking of tribal land, beginning in the late 1800s, was an issue that could not be taken lightly and they filed suit against both the federal government and the state of Washington. Among the lands that were lost was a 50-acre tract taken over by the Port of Tacoma in the 1950s—land that a 1984 Supreme Court ruling said was rightfully the Puyallup's. To avoid further suits and potential damage, President George Bush signed a bill settling Puyallup tribal claims against the federal government. The tribe was paid $77.25 million. Four years later, the Puyallup Tribe would negotiate a settlement with Washington.

The tribe signed the Puyallup Land Claims Settlement Agreement in 1988. The agreement relinquished claims to disputed territories unlawfully taken within reservation borders. While land claims were relinquished, the settlement allowed the tribe to negotiate several management agreements with the state of Washington. The agreement between the Puyallup Tribe and various local governments and communities settled long-standing disputes in several key areas. First, it settled land claims. Submerged lands (owned by non-Indians) in the Puyallup River were transferred to the U.S. government to be held in trust for the Puyallup Indian Tribe and given on-reservation status. This gave the Puyallup Tribe and the United States exclusive regulatory authority under federal environmental laws.[4]

The agreement also resolved tribal-state jurisdiction and police powers. The Puyallup agreed not to exert jurisdiction over non-trust lands—the state of Washington would have that authority. The tribe retained jurisdictional authority over members of the tribe and other Indians in accordance with the Indian Child Welfare Act. Both the tribe and state essentially retained jurisdictional authority over their lands and both are responsible for the cost associated with having authority over such lands.[5]

Indian tribes in the Pacific Northwest have traditionally been concerned with fishing rights. The Puyallup Tribe was concerned with fishery preservation and enhancement. The agreement provided for the identification of sites for the enhancement of facilities for fisheries, and the Puyallup agreed to several construction projects by the Port of Tacoma as long as the construction did not have a severe impact on the fisheries. Developers were required to comply with various technical standards for purposes of protecting fisheries. The agreement also resolved disputes between tribal and commercial fishing industries by means of a navigation agreement. The agreement essentially facilitated communication procedures in vessel traffic lanes and anchor sites.[6]

The terms of the agreement are monitored by the Puyallup Tribal Council. The Puyallup Constitution, approved by the Secretary of the Interior on November 11, 1936, places the management of tribal affairs in the hands of the council, which includes a chairman, a vice-chairman, a treasurer, and a secretary. In addition to operating the marina and Quileute Port Authority, the council is the overseer of all tribal programs.

Many of these programs cover areas that are also administered by the state—such as environmental protection and law enforcement. The council must decide when a greater amount of cooperation with the state is needed. Moreover, while a seemingly comprehensive agreement like the Puyallup Land Claims Settlement would appear to settle all jurisdictional issues, this is not always the case. While there are several areas of agreement and cooperation, there are also areas of disagreement between the state and the tribe.

STATE-TRIBAL RELATIONS

Environmental Management

Air Quality Management

The Puyallup Tribe has its own air quality program that receives support from the EPA. While the tribe does have its own air quality standards, they are basically the same standards set by the state, which has allowed for them to better approach the joint management scheme under which they operate. Prior to the joint management, there were a number of jurisdictional issues that had to be resolved, and conflict occurred more frequently than cooperation. The final incident was a rather minor skirmish that stemmed from the state trying to take action against a tribal member for having an outdoor fire. The tribe asserted their jurisdiction and informed the state that they could not place this individual in the state court system because he was on trust land.[7] The air around the fire was polluted, and both sides realized that the air didn't follow the same rules for jurisdiction that they did. The result was the two sides sitting down to discuss air quality. The tribe really doesn't have a tremendous amount of resources coming from the EPA, and the state generally finds itself short staffed when it comes to environmental management. The problem of jurisdiction and resource deficiencies was resolved through a cooperative agreement, not only with the Puget Sound Air Pollution Control Agency (PSAPCA), but also with the state of Washington Department of Ecology and the EPA. The cooperative agreement established a framework for intergovernmental cooperation and coordination in the development of the Puyallup Tribal Air Quality Program (TAQP). Under this agreement, the PSAPCA provided the tribe with technical and support services in four areas. These areas of support were air quality monitoring program resources; record keeping, such as generation, development, and retrieval of air emissions data; and assisting the tribe regarding development, implementation, and enforcement of permit programs for new and existing air emission sources. The TAQP further coordinated its air quality control program development with the Washington State Implementation Plan to minimize duplication of efforts and monetary expenditures. A Review Advisory Committee was also established. It promoted intergovernmental advocacy and facilitated communication through members of both the TAQP and the PSAPCA who served on the advisory committee.[8]

In addition to the spark from the disputed open fire, the negotiations between the two sides were facilitated by the 1988 land claims settlement, which clarified jurisdictional areas (the tribe did have jurisdiction on the trust area) and also encouraged greater state-tribal cooperation and the forming of joint management agreements. Having the outside push to negotiate a settlement was beneficial in moving the process along and gave both sides the incentive to meet and negotiate in good faith. Another outside aid to the negotiation was the presence of the EPA, which is also a part of the agreement. In the case of air quality management, the relationship was not bad to begin with, and because the state and tribe share the same set of standards, it is possible that some sort of agreement might have emerged anyway given the fact that it saves resources. However, when agencies discuss their roles and their powers, problems are bound to emerge. According to the head of the Puyallup Department of the Environment, without the external pressure of the land claims agreement and the push for cooperation, the process would have been "slow and contentious."[9]

Water Quality Management

In the land claims settlement, the tribe retained the banks of the Puyallup River and anything below the mean high water mark. Because they are downstream from all other parties, they have exclusive jurisdiction over the river—their water standards and treaty rights prevail. The tribe has decided not to adopt state standards for water quality as they did for air quality and has opted for a stricter set of regulations. Since the tribe has stronger, federally promulgated, standards, they have left enforcement authority with the EPA. Since the EPA is the enforcing authority, all suits go through federal courts. While the state and tribe have an agreement for joint air quality management, there is no such agreement for water. Even though there is no formal agreement in place, the tribe and Department of Ecology have been able to maintain a relatively healthy working relationship. This is primarily because both sides, to date, have worked on establishing trust, have realized that it is possible to disagree in a respectful manner and move on, and have recognized that they generally aren't very far apart on most issues.

With higher standards and prevailing water rights, the tribe is largely able to dictate what occurs upstream and is therefore able to regulate the cities of Puyallup and Tacoma. To date, this has not caused any problems, and the state and tribe have not had any major confrontations. There have been some problems with the power industry and the operation of small-scale hydroelectric plants that disrupt the flow rate of the river and have, at times, dropped the river below minimum in-stream flows.[10] The power industry represents a very powerful constituency in the state of Washington and they have influence from the state legislature and governor's office up to Congress. A proposed move by Puget Sound Energy Corporation (Puget Power) may disrupt the positive relations that currently exist between the tribe and state Department of Ecology—and perhaps the tribe and state in other areas.

Puget Power is the largest investor-owned energy corporation in Washington and wields a tremendous amount of political clout. They have decided to go into the water business and have announced plans to withdraw water at 150 cubic feet per second/year from the Puyallup River and sell it out of the stream system. This is of obvious concern for the tribe, who, as the downstream rights holders, will feel any impact from the diminished stream flow. Thus far, the Department of Ecology has been directed to go along with the Puget Power plans and have approved them. The problem is that none of the tribes in Washington have had their water rights adjudicated and the Puyallup Tribe may have claims to enough water to put an end to any upstream diversions. Moreover, the diversions may impact endangered salmon in the river, which will draw the ire of the tribe, sportsmen, and environmentalists. If the plan moves forward there will undoubtedly be a fight, and the tribe will certainly push to have their water rights quantified.

When asked how this would impact the current positive relations between the state and the tribe, the head of the Puyallup Department of the Environment replied, "Basically we drink paper water. As a tribe, we would be happy to get the mean in-stream flow preserved in perpetuity. But this will be an interesting process and a political nightmare."[11] The issue will clearly be divisive and powerful forces are going to mobilize on both sides of the issue. As a politically driven entity, the Department of Ecology will undoubtedly be forced to one side or the other. If the current position of allowing the diversion is maintained, relations with the tribe could suffer.

Law Enforcement

Law enforcement cooperation is another area that has benefited from the jurisdictional clarification that emerged from the land claims settlement. The tribe has sole jurisdiction over its members on trust land and the state has sole jurisdiction over non-trust property. While this provides for clear authority, it also creates a jurisdictional gap—non-natives on trust property. This jurisdictional gap created some very real problems for the state, tribe, and surrounding communities, which eventually led to compromise and cooperation.

During the latter part of the 1980s there was an increase in drug activity on the Puyallup Reservation, which is adjacent to Tacoma and large parts of Pierce County, and is situated right on the I-5 corridor. Many non-members knew that they could come onto trust property and avoid city jurisdiction and as non-natives they also fell outside tribal arrest authority. If the tribe and surrounding law enforcement agencies did not come to some sort of an agreement, the drug problem would continue to escalate.

According to the Director of Puyallup Law Enforcement, "We had a good county sheriff at the time that recognized the problem and said 'hey, let's sit down and fix this.' He was concerned about the community!"[12] In 1991 the tribe and all of the surrounding cities and counties sat down to plug the jurisdictional hole and came away with a cross-commissioning agreement. Through this agreement, the various agencies share information and engage in joint training and work together in cooperative ventures. Each officer is empowered to act as one of his or her counterparts as the need arises. For instance, a tribal officer working in a joint venture has the same arrest authority in the county as does the county officer. The key is that the tribal officer is working as a county officer in that situation and would follow the same laws and procedures that other county officers do. Similarly, an outside law enforcement officer acting in a tribal capacity would follow and respect the rules and procedures set forth by the tribe. They share resources and assist one another in what can only be considered a "win-win for the tribe and surrounding areas."[13]

In this case there was simply a major issue that needed to be addressed. The primary obstacle to the cross-commission was simply a number of questions about how to do it—this was new for all of them. They weren't sure about the legalities and whether or not the blurring/sharing of jurisdiction would be upheld in court (it has been).

Given the glaring hole and rise in drug traffic, however, all of the parties involved were willing to try. The officers and agencies were able to set aside jurisdictional differences and focus on the greater good, which was the community. In the mind of the tribe, sovereignty was not only preserved by sitting down and working out a cross-commissioning agreement, it was enhanced. According to the head of tribal law enforcement,

> The community has to be foremost in the minds of all these agencies—that's the bottom line. There are ways of doing this, and I know that tribes really want to keep their sovereignty intact, and there are ways of doing this which, in my belief not only keeps sovereignty intact but also in some ways strengthens it.[14]

With cooperation there is recognition. While the preservation of sovereign rights sometimes keeps tribes and states from working together, this case illustrates another perspective. In order to cross-commission or work together on a government-to-government basis, there is an inherent recognition of governmental legitimacy. The right to opt into negotiations is the exercise of sovereignty just as much, or more, than attempting to operate independently.

Other Issues

Smoke Shops

There have been a few skirmishes between the state and tribe over tribal smoke shops that sell tobacco products with lower tax rates. The real issues are taxation—whether tribal operations should be taxed by the state—and land use. If truly sovereign, the local land use rules should not apply in Indian country. In 1980 the Supreme Court ruled that states could require tribes to impose state taxes on sales to non-members. The Court did not specify how records were to be kept or how collections were to be made. The ruling, coupled with the logistic realities of enforcing the ruling, has led to conflict across the country. From the Indian-cigarette war of the 1970s, to a military-like raid on the Puyallup Tribe in 1991 (with both federal and state officers leading the way), to questions about whether the city can shut off the utilities to a smoke shop that runs counter to their own land use, smoke shops are an issue that pits states and tribes against one another.[15] At its core, the issue is about sovereignty, and any threat to sovereignty is going to lead to tension. This tension, if left unabated, can have a negative impact on cooperative efforts between states and tribes.

Gaming

Gaming is not so much a problem as it is something that may, in the case of the Puyallup Tribe, lead to positive relations with surrounding communities. Gaming is not something that every tribe should venture into, and it has both positive and negative ramifications for tribes that go well beyond the scope of this discussion. For our purposes, however, gaming has allowed the tribe to share proceeds with other levels of government. Using the definition of cooperation provided by the Chief of the Navajo Police Department—that cooperation is the sharing of resources and respect for another's way of doing things—the Puyallup Tribe is attempting to cooperate with the cities of Fife and Tacoma and Pierce County. In 1998 alone, not long after they opened up a casino (that was only in the planning stages in 1996), the tribe gave $343,788 in grants to these communities for various projects.[16] Such a gesture will hopefully go a long way in solidifying relationships and in building the bridges necessary for intergovernmental cooperation. While gaming has been the root cause of tension for many other tribes and states, it may prove to be a positive here.

SUMMARY AND KEY POINTS

Overall, the level of cooperation between the Puyallup Tribe and the state of Washington is fairly high. More importantly, given the ability of local governments, such as Tacoma, to influence state positions, the tensions between the tribe and surrounding communities have been minimized. The tribe and many of its agencies have been able to negotiate several agreements with the state and most of those involved are beginning to develop a certain level of trust. This trust will be tested as water quantification begins to occur and as Puget Power's plan to withdraw water from the Puyallup River moves closer to becoming a reality. With much of the state's water currently in appropriation, this battle will be fierce. If tensions do arise and threaten the relationship between the tribe and state, hopefully they can draw upon their trust and some of the past tactics they have used in forming this relationship. Among the factors that have assisted the two sides are:

1. The clarification of land claims and jurisdiction—With the assistance of the federal government, the Puyallup Tribe and the state of Washington were able to reach agreement on the 1988 land claims settlement. This single action has largely been responsible for the cooperative efforts undertaken in other areas, such as air quality management and law enforcement. While jurisdictional disputes lie at the heart of failed negotiations in other state-tribal relationships, this issue has been taken off the table for the Puyallup and Washington. While the settlement has some holes to fill, and there will be occasional jurisdictional questions, the initial clarification made it possible for the state and tribe to begin discussions over joint management in several areas. Once the talks began, it was discovered that the two sides were really not that far apart and had similar regulatory standards and legal codes.

2. External guidance can be beneficial—In addition to clarifying jurisdictional areas, the land claims settlement contained provisions that encouraged joint management in several areas. Many times, such an approach is not even considered. With the question of sovereignty at the forefront of people's minds (for both the state and tribe), opportunities for mutual gain can be missed. Having a framework or some source of external guidance that brings sides together without sacrificing sovereignty will certainly be beneficial for states and tribes as they attempt to forge new relationships. External guidance was also demonstrated when the county sheriff initiated discussion on the cross-commissioning agreement. Whether the external force is a visionary individual, a document, or a governmental/agency policy, sometimes negotiations need a push.

3. Take a chance—In many cases, cooperative efforts are avoided simply because it is new territory and the agencies involved do not want to make a mistake. With litigation running rampant in state-tribal relations, and jurisdictional questions lurking around every corner, there is a tendency to accept the status quo—even when things can clearly be improved. In the case of the cross-commissioning agreement between the tribe and other law enforcement agencies, this was completely uncharted territory for all of them. According to the head of tribal law enforcement, the biggest obstacle was the fear of not knowing how to do it. All of the officers knew there was a jurisdictional gap that needed to be plugged, and the community was suffering as a result, but they had no prior history with cross-commissioning. They worked out the details, implemented the plan, and waited to see if it would work or hold up in court. It was an operational and legal success and has been a win-win for all of the communities. They took a chance and it paid off.

4. Recognize sovereignty—Sovereignty is something that can never be ignored when dealing with government-to-government cooperation. If the rights of one side are diminished, true cooperation and joint efforts have not been achieved. Too often, states and tribes feel that in order to assert their sovereignty, they must avoid cooperation and must, instead, take a confrontational/adversarial position. In some cases, this is true. If an agreement is one-sided and diminishes sovereignty, this type of arrangement should be contested—by either side. However, as the head of law enforcement for the Puyallup Tribe rightly points out, the act of cooperation is also the assertion of sovereignty. To enter into a mutually beneficial arrangement on a government-to-government basis—as equals—inherently recognizes sovereignty and the right to govern one's own people.

5. The importance of trust and time—While the land claims settlement has only been active for twenty years, which is a relatively short time when looking at historic relations, this has provided the opportunity for the state and tribe to engage in a number of cooperative ventures. During this period, both sides have been able to see that they have gained from the experience and that the other side is not automatically looking for an angle from which to harm the other at a later date. In other words, they are beginning to develop a level of trust (which could be viewed as a certain degree of predictability). While they do not cooperate on every issue, they no longer automatically shy away from collaboration.

The relations between states and tribes have developed over a long period of time and have tended to erode, rather than build, trust. It will take time for bridges to be built and for both sides to get to a point where they are actually dealing with one another without inherent skepticism. While the trust that the Puyallup and Washington have started to develop will be tested with the water issue, hopefully they have built up enough positive experiences that they can withstand the blow and move forward in a productive manner.

NOTES

1. Washington Governor's Office of Indian Affairs, http://www.goia.wa.gov/tribalinfo/puyallup.html.
2. Ibid.
3. U.S. Department of Commerce, *American Indian Reservation and Indian Trust Areas* (Washington, D.C.: U.S. Government Printing Office, 1996).
4. M. O'Connell, interview by Secody Hubbard, personal interview, July 1995.
5. B. K. Gover et al., "Tribal-State Dispute Resolution: Recent Attempts," *South Dakota Law Review* 36 (1991), pp. 277–98.
6. Ibid.
7. William Sullivan, interview by Jeff Ashley, telephone interview, July 2002, on file with author.
8. A. Bryant, interview by Secody Hubbard, personal interview, December 1995.
9. Sullivan, interview.
10. Ibid.
11. Ibid.
12. Rory LaDucer, interview by Jeff Ashley, telephone interview, July 2002, on file with author.
13. Ibid.
14. Ibid.
15. See Dan Hannula, "Did State Double-Cross Puyallup Tribe?," *Seattle Times*, 27 November 1991; and Stephen Clutter, "Smoke Shop Breaks Pact, Government Officials Fume," *Seattle Times*, 11 January 1996.
16. "Puyallup Tribe Will Award Grants to Cities and County," *Seattle Post-Intelligencer*, 17 September 1998.

CHAPTER 7

The Confederated Salish-Kootenai Tribes of the Flathead Nation

The Flathead Indian Reservation is home to three separate but consolidated tribes—the Salish, Pend d'Oreille, and the Kootenai. All three tribes were inhabitants of the Montana territory well in advance of any European incursion. In fact, many archaeologists believe that the Kootenai may have lived in the area for thousands of years. The Salish are believed to have migrated to the area from the Columbia Plateau, but have still called Montana home for several hundred years.[1] Both tribes are part of the Salishan language group, which also includes the Pend d'Oreille and Kalispell tribes.

While there were undoubtedly several contacts between the Salishan tribes and European trappers, the first major contact came after the Louisiana Purchase of 1803. The Lewis and Clark expedition, which was charged with exploring the territory for the U.S. government, worked its way into Montana in 1805. Upon entering the territory, the group of explorers noted that the Salishan tribes spoke a language that was quite unlike any other that they had encountered before. They also found the tribes to be incredibly hospitable. The expedition had previously attempted to travel to the Salmon River and through Lost Trail Pass, but was unable to accomplish their goal despite several attempts. They finally managed to meet the challenge with directions from the Salish, who knew the area. The tribes were also willing to share food with members of the expedition. Since game was scarce in the mountains, and the explorers were running low on food, this gesture was monumental for the Lewis and Clark group.[2]

Shortly after the Lewis and Clark expedition passed through, François

Antoine Laroque explored the Yellowstone River for the North West Company of Canada. It was becoming apparent that some of the rivers in the area were growing into major travel routes for both tribes and early explorers. In 1807—only two years after the Lewis and Clark expedition—a trading post was set up by a group of people who traveled up the Missouri River from St. Louis. The conflict between the tribes and white settlers was inevitable—not all newcomers were as peaceful and accepting as the Lewis and Clark team apparently was.[3] The inflow of white traders, trappers, and settlers increased rather rapidly as the early fur traders opened up more and more territory. The abundance of beaver in the lakes and streams attracted corporations such as the North West Company and the American Fur Company to the area—bringing yet more people and more trading posts. The fur trade would begin to wane in the 1840s, but a presence was already felt. Moreover, as fur was diminishing in importance, a new attraction would bring even more people into the area (and into conflict with the tribes)—gold.

The northwestern portion of what is now Montana was the subject of the Oregon Treaty of 1846 between the United States and the British. While there had been some growth and settlement because of the fur trade, the region was still primarily wilderness. However, the discovery of gold in 1852 would bring on a period of rapid growth. Those searching for instant wealth were different than the trappers and were much more boisterous and confrontational. It was during this period that the United States realized that the Indians of Montana could not be ignored. Following the traditional pattern of land grabbing and paternalism (the idea being that the Indians needed to be protected from the onslaught of miners), the government and several tribes—among them the Salish, Kootenai, and Pend d'Oreilles—entered into the treaty of Hell Gate in 1855.[4]

The Flathead Indian Reservation is located in the northwestern part of Montana. The reservation was established by the Hell Gate Treaty of July 16, 1855, which ceded most of Montana to the United States in exchange for 1,234,969 acres. A succession of acts (most notably the Dawes Act) that dissipated tribal holdings through land allotment and non-Indian homesteading followed. About one-half of the land within the reservation, including almost all of the better agricultural land located in the valley bottoms, is non-Indian-owned. The mountains, upland range, and valuable forest lands are Indian-owned. The combination of fee land and tribally owned land has led to many of the tensions plaguing several tribes who have both members and non-members living within reservation borders.

Today the Flathead Reservation, located on the western slope of the Rocky Mountains in western Montana, is home to roughly 4,000 Salish, Kootenai, and Pend d'Oreille. The tribal government consists of a 10-member tribal council elected from 5 districts. Five members are elected to 4-year terms in biennial elections. Following the election, a chairman and vice-chairman are chosen by the council, and a secretary and treasurer are selected at large by the council. This body oversees the operation of tribal programs.

STATE-TRIBAL RELATIONS

Environmental Management

Air Quality Management

The current tribal air-quality program was developed in 1979 as a result of efforts to reclassify the reservation's airshed from class two to class one. Thus, the tribe has a well established program and has developed their own set of air quality standards. While initially receptive to tribal authority (when money was available), the state cooled to cooperative efforts when state dollars were involved.

Of the tribes studied, the conflicting nature of jurisdiction is historically the most intense in the case of the Confederated Salish and Kootenai Tribes of the Flathead Nation in the state of Montana. The jurisdictional confrontation on the Flathead Indian Reservation stems from the Dawes Act of 1887, which eventually led to the opening of reservation lands to non-Indian settlements in 1910. The tribes hold 60 percent of the land base, but the remaining 40 percent is fee property. The 2000 census reveals that roughly 65 percent of the population within the exterior boundaries of the reservation are non-Indian. Since the majority of the population is non-Indian (this segment is well represented in the Montana state government), the tribes reported that they encounter strong opposition from the non-Indian occupants on the reservation. Essentially, these occupants refuse to recognize and accept that the Flathead Nation has jurisdiction within its own reservation boundaries. In 1988, the Division of Environmental Protection for the tribes, recognizing the strong opposition to tribal regulatory authority on their lands, initiated contact with the city mayors of Ronan and Polson to establish steering committees to address the concerns of both non-Indians and Indians regarding air quality. These committees worked well for a period of time until grant funds to the tribe from the EPA were cut, and both communities basically lost contact and communication.

In 1995 the tribal EPA staff, despite the controversial issues surrounding the jurisdiction, reported that a Memorandum of Agreement (MOA) had actively been sought for approximately eight months with the city of Polson, Montana, without results. The impasse could only be attributed to the lack of funding and disagreement regarding tribal jurisdiction. The tribal, state, and local government conflicts were rather fierce, with litigation rather than negotiation the norm. As a result of ongoing litigation, ties between the governments were severed.[5]

The relations between the state, tribe, and surrounding regions in the area of air quality management have improved somewhat since 1995. Things are not nearly as adversarial as they once were. For a time, the state had wanted control. Recently the tribe has not experienced any state encroachment in that area. This is partly because the state lacks the resources to adequately enforce their regulations on tribal lands. The autonomy of the tribal program is actually something of a relief because state funds can be devoted elsewhere. EPA money has led to something of a convenient recognition of sovereignty and authority. While the basic beliefs of tribal and state officials do not appear to have changed much over time, their actions have become more accepting. Relations have clearly gotten better—while there are no cooperative efforts, there is no open antagonism and the basic approach is jurisdictional separation. According to air quality manager Randy Ashley, "now when people call the state, the state replies that they are hands off—that anything on reservation is in the hands of the tribe."[6]

Relations have also improved slightly since 1995 because there have been two face to face meetings involving state, tribal, and federal officials. In the case of the two sides sitting down at the table, it was the Bureau of Land Management (BLM) that brought the two sides together. The BLM was meeting with the state and the EPA when someone among them recognized that the tribes were noticeably absent and extended an invitation for them to join the discussion. The parties had a roundtable discussion that allowed for a better understanding of the people, interests, and issues. There have been no formal agreements as a result of these meetings, and only two meetings have been held since 1995, but it is certainly a start. One major point that became obvious in the meetings is that the technical people share a similar set of core beliefs.

As with many other tribes, jurisdictional disputes and politics seem to be the major obstacles to formalizing any cooperative efforts. "The people who work in the field get along very well. It's when you get into upper management and upper administration that there's conflict."[7] The tribal air quality manager sees no obstacles to forming an MOU at a technical level but does not see anything happening anytime soon. "Someone would just have to sit down and write it. Although one obstacle is that politically such an agreement would require the state acknowledging tribal sovereignty."[8] The fear is that cooperation in one area might be used against the tribe in another. This is a big concern with pending water rights litigation and points to the fact that—at least in this relationship—issues cannot be separated. According to the head of the tribal air program, "Until water rights are settled, we won't see an MOU for air."

Water Quality Management

One of the biggest issues facing the state of Montana and the Salish-Kootenai tribe is the quantification of water rights. While many of the other tribes in the state have settled long-standing water rights disputes, the Salish-Kootenai feel that the settlement agreements gave up too much in the way of Indian reserved rights. While some of the other tribes were willing to concede that the waters running through the reservation were not theirs, this is something the Salish-Kootenai will not do. They claim 100 percent ownership of these waters and the state is not pleased. The issue is currently under litigation and the cloud over water rights hinders any moves toward water quality cooperation (and perhaps other areas of environmental management).[9]

There are no formal mechanisms for state-tribal cooperation in the area of water quality management and there are no MOUs or MOAs. Such an approach is not even being considered at this time. The relationship between the state and tribe, at least for environmental issues, seems to be more of a hands-off strict separation of jurisdictions approach rather than a cooperative resource and information sharing approach. This is particularly true for water. There appear to be three main reasons why the state and the tribe cannot negotiate water quality agreements. First, there is the fear, on both sides, that any agreements that are not very carefully scrutinized might become precedent setting and be used against them in other areas (such as water rights). The other two reasons are the presence of the EPA and what is perceived to be the remnants of long-term confusion about the tribal status in the state.

Montana is one of the states people think of as the old West. Unfortunately, the cowboy mentality, or the perception that it exists, can spoil attempts to move the two sides together. Signs that proudly discuss the founding of surrounding cities without mention of the fact that there were once other people who lived there do not help. Many people in Montana, including non-natives living on the reservation, have a hard time accepting the legitimacy of the tribe. It is hard to negotiate when the two sides have had such different experiences. Not everyone on the state side knows what it is like to live with prejudice. The Salish people were force marched off of their land by the ancestors of the state people. While that was long ago, some prejudice still exists and relations are going to suffer. It seems that in this particular area—water—relations are the worst. Perhaps this is because the public has never been informed about the legal/political status of tribes and the history behind that status. The fact that there are no clear guidelines or definitions to follow makes such a lack of education even more problematic. According to a representative from the Salish-Kootenai water program, "There needs to be a clear definition of Indian country—it seems to change from place to place and makes for confusion. Sometimes this is a ruse—state people saying we don't know what that is. The result is a series of legal battles to prove tribal existence and jurisdiction."[10] The general feeling is that a lack of precise guidelines and uniform definitions of Indian country allows for people to make mistakes or intentionally (when it is politically beneficial) feign confusion over tribal sovereign rights and jurisdiction. Regardless, the result has been a great deal of litigation, an adversarial process that is not conducive to positive relations.

The tribal water program has made an effort to meet with the people in various state programs, but no relationships have been established and no face to face communication has occurred. Part of the problem lies in the fact that this is new territory and nobody knows how to respond. The tribe does not have a set of guidelines or policies for dealing with the state, and the state has no uniform set of rules for interacting with the tribes. A tribal water representative feels that without a directive from the state that mandates interaction and spells out precisely how this interaction should occur, there will be no progress. In a similar vein, no similar directives or guidelines are coming from the tribal council. The feeling is that nobody in the lower levels of the bureaucracy—on either side—wants to make the first move because they are afraid of being reprimanded.[11]

In addition to potential feelings that the tribe is not a legitimate force and the institutional divisions separating the state and tribe in the quest for water quality cooperation, the strict jurisdictional separation of the two sides is actually reinforced by the presence of the EPA. While the EPA has provided the necessary funds and technical training for the tribe to establish and operate its own water program, they have also cut the state out of the process. If the tribe has autonomy and the EPA has full enforcement authority, there is no reason for the tribe to negotiate and deal with the state. If the tribe feels that cooperation is unwelcome, or if they do not welcome state assistance, the ability to handle things independently allows them to forgo cooperating with the state.

Law Enforcement

Unlike the environment, law enforcement offers a good example of cooperation between the tribe, state, and surrounding communities. The level of cooperation between the Salish-Kootenai and law enforcement agencies is among the most positive of the tribes we studied. Not only has the state retro ceded authority that was lost after the passing of PL 280 in the 1950s, but the tribe has entered into formal agreements with the state highway patrol, three surrounding cities, and three of the four counties that touch part of the reservation. Given the anti-tribal sentiment that exists along with the severe checkerboarding and close proximity to several other subnational governments, such cooperation is quite an accomplishment.

The first step toward cooperation was clearly the retro ceding that took place in 1994. While the initial motivation may have been purely economic, the result was an inherent recognition of sovereignty—something that seems to be at the heart of any cooperative effort regardless of the state, tribe, or issue. The retro cession was pushed for two primary reasons—economics and effectiveness. It had become apparent that zero tribal authority over their own members was leading to a number of problems. The biggest problem, from both a state and tribal standpoint, was that a disproportionate number of tribal members were going to prison for minor offenses that escalated into more serious crimes such as resisting arrest and assault. Many of the Indian offenders felt they were being singled out by the white officers and they rebelled—only to find themselves facing long sentences. Not only were tribal members being sent away for crimes that were initially relatively minor, the state had to find prison space for them and tax dollars for their upkeep. The idea behind retro cession was that the tribe would be in the best position to handle their own offenders and de-escalate volatile situations. In addition, since many of the initial crimes involved were alcohol or drug related (such as DUI), there was the recognition that the tribe had more resources to offer in the way of counseling and treatment, which allowed for options not available to the state. The retro cession was a win-win. The state was able to eliminate a number of minor criminals from their prisons and save money. The tribe was able to regain some of its inherent sovereignty and provide more viable options for some of its members.[12] Now the state and tribe have jurisdiction over tribal members for felonies—the tribe has sole jurisdiction for misdemeanors. With the increased authority and sovereignty, the tribe was able to forge cooperative relationships with other governmental agencies.

The tribes have signed agreements with most of the surrounding communities (three cities and three counties) and with the state highway patrol. If one of those agencies stops a tribal member for a misdemeanor (such as DUI) they contact the tribal police who either come to the scene or authorize the non-tribal officer to make the arrest if necessary. If it is a case of writing a citation and releasing the suspect, he or she is cited into tribal court. The same procedure works for tribal police stopping non-members. According to an official with the tribe, "It works pretty well."

For felonies, since jurisdiction is shared, the tribal prosecutor and county prosecutor sit down and decide which justice system makes the most sense on a case-by-case basis. Often, stronger, more serious cases will go to the county or state because the tribal system is limited in the length of sentence to one year in tribal jail versus a lengthy stay in prison. Giving the case over to the state does not tend to alienate the many tribal members who are in favor of sending the more serious criminals away to prison.

It is important to note, once again, that, although the reservation is checkerboarded, the cooperation makes this almost a non-issue with governmental agencies. The key point in the agreements and in the relationship is that they share resources and are respectful of each other's systems. The initial problem was with non-natives who were afraid of the increased police authority of tribal police. They didn't understand and feared anything being supported by the tribe. Since retro cession and the enactment of the cooperative agreements, however, many realize they have actually gained and will call the tribal police first because they are the closest—the county can take over if necessary. Before, the tribal police wouldn't have taken the call because there would have been nothing that they could do.

The agreements were made possible, in large part, because of support coming from Sanders and Missoula Counties. In the case of Sanders County, a relatively small county with few resources, they were calling on the tribal police for support and backup a good deal of the time prior to the actual agreement. Missoula County may have been even more influential as a larger county. They are located at the edge of the reservation and didn't have people stationed that far out at the edge of the county—again, they were relying quite a bit on the tribal police. It simply made sense to formalize the agreements. With these two counties leading the way, the others followed. The key to the negotiations over the formal agreement was keeping things focused only on criminal law enforcement. According to an official with the tribe, "Other areas like game and fish and water are tense so we kept their issues out of it. If we would have added water rights or any of the other stuff into this agreement, I don't think it would have gone."[13]

Other Issues

Taxation

While tribal smoke shops tend to draw the most attention when it comes to state-tribal relations and the issue of taxation, other enterprises can be equally contentious. In the case of the state of Montana and the Confederated Salish-Kootenai Tribes, there has recently been a great deal of attention placed on the state lodging tax. While court rulings have specified that states can require the imposition of state tax on non-Indians who conduct business on the reservation, they have not given the state any specific collection mechanism. The tribe, as a sovereign, feels they are not obligated to serve as a collection arm for the state. At the center of the tension is KwaTaqNuk Resort on Flathead Lake, a 112-room operation. In an attempt to force the tribe to collect the 4 percent state tax, the state filed suit and asked the courts to intervene on its behalf. Thus far, the courts have ruled in favor of the tribe and have stated that while the state is entitled to the tax revenue, it is beyond the authority of the court to order tribal compliance. The tribe is willing to collect for the state, but insist that they need to enter into a formal agreement between sovereign governments—something that the two sides had done once before. In the past, the tribe collected the tax and placed it into a special account—an escrow account—and turned the money over to the state as part of a 1997 agreement. Since turning over the money in July 1997, however, the tribe has refused to collect any state taxes until another—more permanent—arrangement can be negotiated. To date, the state has decided that litigation is preferable to negotiation and has continued to file suit. Given the adversarial nature of such an approach, the relationship between the state and tribe cannot help but suffer.[14]

Game and Fish/Wilderness Preservation

An October 3, 1999, *Las Vegas-Journal Review* headline read "New Battles Ahead Over American Indian Sovereignty." In this article the author discusses many issues that face the Salish-Kootenai and asserts that "tribal sovereignty is an everyday and often fractious struggle."[15] While the author discusses violations of the federal trust responsibility and battles over gaming and taxation, one issue serves as the centerpiece of the article— game and fish regulations. This is an often contentious issue that led to armed conflict in Wisconsin. Fortunately no shots have been fired on the Flathead Reservation, but there is tension brewing. Most upset are the resident non-members who are barred from hunting big game on tribal land. They live there, and are governed by the tribe, but they do not get to participate in tribal government and have no voice in tribal matters.[16] Although discussed less often than other issues, this is an aspect of the checkerboarding that plagues many reservations. It is also a part of sovereignty and the legal right of tribes to control what happens in their reservations.

In order to preserve the sovereign right, and to preserve cultural integrity, the Salish-Kootenai Tribes entered into an agreement with the state of Montana. This agreement provided the framework for managing wildlife and regulating hunting by non-members. It also implied, to some, that the tribe would not close off other areas of the reservation as long as the agreement was in effect.

Early in 1999, the tribe announced that it was closing four popular recreational areas and that these sites would only be accessible to tribal members. There have always been secluded areas that were off limits to non-natives, but the tribe felt that further closures were necessary to protect the cultural well-being of the tribe. Most notably the tribe wanted to preserve enough space so that tribal members could enjoy a certain amount of solitude and so that they could lessen the chance of their members running into conflict with non-members. Once again the action aggravated non-tribal members and some began to write letters to the Lake County Commission to ask for their help. The commission, in turn, sought to have the state intervene by asserting that such closures were a violation of the game and fish agreement.[17] This is a good illustration of how tribal actions become politicized and the state and tribe are often placed at odds through seemingly benign actions.

A not so benign action that may strain relations between the state and tribe is the result of a court ruling that places further game and fish agreements at risk. In 1999 the Supreme Court ruled that, despite opposition by the Minnesota Department of Game and Fish, the Mille Lacs Band of Chippewa could hunt and fish outside of their reservation boundaries as a treaty protected right that could not be infringed upon by the state. The not so benign move on the part of the Salish-Kootenai was to proclaim that the ruling served as "reaffirmation of the lasting vitality of the Hell Gate Treaty," which was signed before Montana became a state. The tribe added that they "may not now need a hunting and fishing agreement with the state."[18] Whether they did or not, such a proclamation and open challenge may not have been in the best interest of future state-tribal relations—certainly not in the area of game and fish.

SUMMARY AND KEY POINTS

When looking at the relationship and extent of cooperative efforts between the Salish-Kootenai tribes and the state of Montana, it becomes clear that, at least in this case, the specific issue and the individuals involved matter quite a bit. While there is some resemblance to the other cases, this truly is a mixed bag. Law enforcement arrangements are extremely solid and are among the most cooperative we encountered. Air quality management tends to be less cooperative, but still cordial—it is basically a split existence with a hands-off approach on either side. This is an improvement over past relations, which were more contentious and centered around jurisdictional disputes, but still not terribly cooperative. Water issues are heated and the relations are antagonistic. This is primarily because the Salish-Kootenai do not believe a proposed water rights settlement is in their interests and will not sign the accord in its present form. When discussing water, people automatically think of quantity, and any attempts to work cooperatively on water quality will be set aside until the water rights (quantity) are resolved. Adding to the strain are the actions of both the state and tribe in other areas. The tribe has publicly announced that a current negotiated agreement with the state may not be needed in the future (game and fish), and the state has continuously taken the tribe to court over the issue of tax revenue. The higher level politicos are beginning to back each other into a corner over jurisdiction, which will hamper negotiations and cooperation at lower levels.

The experiences of the Salish-Kootenai and the state of Montana offer us both good and bad examples of cooperative efforts. Some of the players involved have provided the following suggestions for improvement.

1. Clear definition of Indian Country—As with other checkerboarded areas, there seems to be a lack of certainty over who is able to do what. In more contentious relationships, as this has historically been, the confusion allows for dispute and inaction. Depending on the issue, either side can simply claim jurisdiction, refuse to compromise, and end the discussion. Quite often these are the issues that end up in court. The case by case judicial defining of Indian Country is not conducive to cooperative relationships. This needs to be resolved before any true communication and cooperation can occur on a regular basis.

2. Let the common good be the driving force and stay focused—Despite the severe checkerboarding that has hampered overall state-tribal relations, the level of cooperation between law enforcement agencies at all levels of government is very high. These agencies have been able to work around the issue of jurisdiction and have developed a way for them all to share resources and better serve the communities they are in place to protect. Ignoring the jurisdictional lines and allowing for officers (regardless of agency) to enforce the law in a timely manner has been of benefit to everyone. The cooperation has worked so well that even those who were initially opposed (mostly resident non-natives) are pleased with the cooperative result.

    In negotiating the cooperative agreements, it was essential that the agencies stay focused on the single issue of criminal law enforcement. They all had a desire to make their communities safer, but the discussion would have ended if they had strayed into areas such as game and fish and water.

3. A framework for lower levels to follow—There should be a guiding principle or policy (on both sides) that dictates how lower level bureaucrats should interact. More importantly, such a policy should mandate that discussions and cooperation occur. Often, especially when it is clear that higher level relations are hostile, those in the trenches feel that interaction and discussion will result in reprimand. The technical people need to be assured that collaboration and cooperation is not only supported, but it is encouraged. Then, they need to be given a rough framework to follow so that this can actually occur. This is the same approach that led to a number of positive agreements between the Navajo Nation and the ADEQ.

4. External support and third parties are helpful—The power of allies and neutral third parties cannot be overstated. The strong cooperative agreement and sharing of resources in law enforcement was made a reality by having two of the surrounding counties champion the cause. Missoula County has a certain amount of political power and their support was very important when attempting to get the state and other counties to sign off on the agreement. Another

area where a third party can be helpful is with the air quality relationship. Like water, the relationship between the state and tribe has historically been hostile. This has changed since the BLM suggested that the tribe be brought into management discussions with the EPA and the state. Without this external force, the state and tribe might have never met face to face and had the opportunity to simply talk. The two discussions allowed both sides to share information and to find out more about what the other did and how they did it. What they found was that they were not that far apart and that they shared a set of core values and goals—a crucial first step if they are ever to enter into formal cooperative efforts.

NOTES

1. http://www.lewisandclark.state.mt.us/salish.htm.
2. Ibid.
3. "Early Inhabitants, Fur Trading, and Gold," http://www.factmonster.com/ce6/us/A0859754.html.
4. Ibid. See http://www.skc.edu/atd/hellgate.htm for the actual treaty. In the treaty it is interesting to note that the Salish were referred to as the Flathead. Early settlers had called them this because they mistakenly believed that the tribe engaged in the practice of head flattening.
5. Lewis Mcload, interview by Secody Hubbard, personal interview, 1995.
6. Randy Ashley, interview by Jeff Ashley, telephone interview, June 2002, on file with author.
7. Ibid.
8. Ibid.
9. Randy Ashley and anonymous tribal water quality representative, interview by Jeff Ashley, telephone interview, June 2002, on file with author.
10. Tribal water quality representative, interview.
11. Ibid.
12. Les Clairmont, interview by Jeff Ashley, telephone interview, June 2002, on file with author.
13. Ibid.
14. See "Sovereignty Issue Cuts Lake County Bed Tax," Associated Press State and Local Wire, 24 March 1999; "State Sues Over Tribal Resort's Refusal to Impose Bed Tax," Associated Press State and Local Wire, 9 October 2000; and "Judge Tosses Suit Over Tribal Resort Collecting Lodging Tax," Associated Press State and Local Wire, 28 February 2001.
15. Jim Nesbitt, "New Battles Ahead Over American Indian Sovereignty," *Las Vegas-Journal Review-Journal*, 3 October 1999.
16. Ibid.
17. "Salish-Kootenai Propose Closing Tribal Recreation Areas to Non-Members," Associated Press State and Local Wire, 20 April 1999.
18. "Pablo: Supreme Court Decision Reinforces Indian Fishing Rights in Montana," Associated Press State and Local Wire, 29 March 1999.

CHAPTER 8

The Shoshone-Bannock Tribes

The people who live on the Fort Hall Indian Reservation are direct descendants of native people who once freely moved about through portions of what are now Wyoming, Utah, Nevada, and Idaho. It is believed that the Shoshone were the first of the two to arrive and inhabited most of what is now Idaho for several hundred years before any European contact. The Bannock (previously called Northern Paiute) arrived sometime during the 1700s. The introduction of horses in the early 1700s allowed some groups of Shoshone and Bannock to travel even greater distances in search of buffalo and other game.[1] The people were able to hunt, gather, and fish for salmon without much outside interference. This went on for an extended period of time and clearly predates any thoughts of a U.S. government or the state of Idaho.

Much like their neighbors to the west, the Salish and Kootenai, the first outsiders they encountered were trappers and explorers. Also mirroring the Salish-Kootenai experience, the first significant contact with the U.S. government came after the Louisiana Purchase of 1803. The Lewis and Clark expedition made its way into Idaho not long after their encounters with the Indians of Montana. Upon entering the territory, the explorers noted that the Salishan tribes spoke a language that was quite unlike any other that they had encountered before. They also found the tribes to be friendly. While the dialect of the Shoshone and Bannock differed from the Salishan (the Shoshone and Bannock descend from the Numic family of the Uto-Aztecan linguistic phylum), they were just as hospitable as their Montana neighbors.[2] In fact, when most people think of the interactions between the Lewis and Clark expedition and American Indians, the name

Sacajawea inevitably comes up. Sacajawea is famous for serving as a guide for the expedition and assisting them in their travels west to the Pacific Ocean. This famous woman also happens to have been Shoshone.

After the expedition had departed, the Shoshone and Bannock (Paiute) continued to forage for food and to hunt buffalo, which was of both cultural and nutritional importance. The continued contact with trappers and traders did little to disrupt them. Unfortunately, the fur trade had almost ended by 1840 and the Hudson Bay Company controlled most of the region. The company shifted attention away from the fur trade to the business of setting up outposts to serve (and thereby facilitate) the increasing number of settlers heading west. Among the posts established by the company were Fort Hall and Fort Boise. Fort Hall, founded in 1834, was located right along the Oregon Trail and was an important supply and rest stop for the continuous stream of Europeans. The swelling tide of immigration that was in progress disrupted the Shoshone-Bannock homelands and way of life. Buffalo herds began to diminish and hunting patterns were disrupted. As food supplies became less abundant and their culture began to suffer, many Shoshone and Bannock grew to resent the intruders but could do little to stop them.[3]

Things only got worse for the Shoshone and Bannock. A series of Idaho gold rushes brought even more settlers to the region, and the widespread slaughter of the buffalo for sport was seriously undermining the tribes' traditional lifestyle. A major mineral discovery in 1860 pushed the U.S. government to act. The government and the two tribes entered into the Treaty of Soda Springs in the mid-1800s, but the treaty was never ratified by Congress. The tribes and the government then negotiated a second treaty—the 1868 Treaty of Fort Bridger—which was ratified. The Treaty of Fort Bridger established the Fort Hall Reservation.[4]

The Fort Hall Reservation was established with 1.8 million acres set aside for tribal use. Unfortunately, a survey error in 1872 reduced the size of the reservation to 1.2 million acres—a loss of roughly one-third. This was only the beginning of the land loss that the Shoshone and Bannock would face at the hands of both the United States and the state of Idaho and surrounding communities. The city of Pocatello actually stemmed from a railroad station located on the reservation, but quickly grew in size and pushed for more territory. The tribes were forced to negotiate a land deal with the city around the turn of the century. In return for approximately $600,000, the tribe gave up 420,000 acres of land to accommodate the growth of Pocatello. Eager settlers took part in the "Day of the Run" on June 7, 1902, when six thousand settlers ran across the soil and laid claim to what was formerly tribal land.[5]

The Dawes Act would result in the loss of even more tribal land. Between 1911 and 1913 alone over 347,000 acres of reservation land had been broken up and offered as individual allotments. Of this, roughly 36,000 acres left tribal hands. The Indian Reorganization Act would later help to remedy some of the excesses of allotment, but over time the size of the reservation was cut considerably. Originally promised close to 2 million acres (1.8 million), the tribes were left with substantially less.[6]

Today, the reservation is situated in southeastern Idaho and consists of 546,000 acres, with 96 percent of this land owned by individual members and the tribe. Over 120,000 acres of the reservation is farmed (potatoes and grain). The reservation is located along the Snake River plain, the major watershed in southern Idaho, and extends to Bannock, Bingham, Caribou, and Power Counties. The reservation is positioned along a major highway and is situated between two mid-sized college towns—Pocatello and Idaho Falls. The crosscutting of the highway and the positioning creates a certain amount of jurisdictional tension.

Tribes on the Fort Hall Reservation are organized as a sovereign government that uses money generated through a variety of endeavors such as agriculture, tourism, and other business enterprises to support programs for both members and non-members. The reservation and the government are led by the Fort Hall Tribal Council. The Tribal Council (also called the Fort Hall Business Council) consists of seven elected members, who are the official governing body of the Shoshone-Bannock Tribes. The Tribes are federally recognized and both are organized under the Indian Reorganization Act (IRA) of 1934. A tribal constitution and by-laws were adopted and approved by the Secretary of the Interior in 1936. All programs and proposed cooperative efforts with the state of Idaho must go through the council.

STATE-TRIBAL RELATIONS

Environmental Management

The Fort Hall Land Use Department was established by the tribes for the control and protection of all lands and natural resources on the reservation. In 1974 the Tribes passed the Tribal Environmental Policy Act (TEPA), a broad legislative-like ordinance designed to advance the programs and regulations that protect human health and the environment. The Land Use Ordinance was adopted in 1979, the first such comprehensive ordinance to be adopted by any American Indian tribe. A three-member elected body of commissioners develops and oversees the land use policies of the reservation, while a Land Use Director manages and coordinates the various staff and programs within the department. The ordinance was established to safeguard and promote the peace, safety, morals, and general welfare of all who may choose to reside within the reservation. This mandate allowed the Land Use Department to manage environmental protection programs for the Shoshone-Bannock people.

The pesticide program, hazardous waste, water, air, and off-reservation environmental protection programs are all presently operational within the Land Use Department.[7]

Air Quality Management

The southwestern part of the Fort Hall Reservation has been designated by the EPA as a non-attainment area for particulate matter of less than ten (10) micrometers in aerodynamic diameter (PM-10). Particulate matter is a health concern because it may enter the lungs and cause reduced lung function and respiratory illness. The primary sources of particulate matter are phosphorous industry releases, agriculture, and road dust.

The Tribes have established an Air Quality Program and have developed a program to control air pollution on the reservation. The Fort Hall Business Council passed the Air Quality Protection Act in 1992 and the Tribal Air Quality Rules & Regulations in August 1993. One of the ways to control air pollution is through a Tribal Implementation Plan (TIP), which places various controls on air emission sources in order to reduce the PM-10 levels on the reservation. The Tribal Air Quality Program has developed a TIP and other regulations to bring the Fort Hall Reservation into compliance with national standards. The air quality program has established its own standards and handles its own monitoring, testing, and enforcement without any state assistance.

Sho-Ban Air Quality Control currently does not have an intergovernmental agreement or a memorandum of understanding with state or local governments in Idaho. From 1989 through 1993 a Memorandum of Agreement (MOA) was negotiated with the state of Idaho allowing joint permitting of major polluters on the reservation; however, the agreement was canceled by the tribe because of differing perspectives on cooperation. The tribe felt that the former MOA benefited the state more than the tribe and that the tribe was never viewed as an equal partner. This stemmed from the belief that the MOA was never executed in a fashion that reflected a recognition of the tribes' authority to regulate and that there was inadequate recognition of what the tribes wanted in the area of enforcement and air quality control. According to Roger Turner of the Shoshone-Bannock Air Quality Program, "We didn't think the job was getting done to the satisfaction of the tribes. There wasn't a great deal of enforcement and there was the general feeling that the tribe could handle the issue more effectively themselves."[8] The program was able to break from the state because of a financial commitment from the tribe and funding from the EPA. The federal agency also provides some technical assistance.

Since the breakdown of the MOA, relations with the state have actually improved, as the tribe has proven itself to be technically and financially capable of doing things without the state of Idaho. The conflict has also been lessened because the regulatory atmosphere has changed as the result of two important federal actions. The first was the tribal authority rule in the federal register, which outlines how tribes can gain Clean Air Act authority. The Shoshone-Bannock tribe followed this procedure and gained authority as a state under the Clean Air Act. The second action was the EPA providing a direct method to permit emissions sources on reservations through the part 71 permitting process (CAA sect 71), which provides the EPA with direct authority to permit major emission sources. These two things have left the Shoshone-Bannock in a strong position relative to the state. According to Turner, "The tribe does things on their own or holding hands with the EPA—the tribe just feels more comfortable working with the federal regulatory folks than they do with the state."[9]

One problem is the question of jurisdiction over fee land. While the tribes own 96 percent of the land and do not suffer from the same problems as do other tribes, there have been some questions. For example, two smelters are the primary sources of pollution for the reservation—Astaris and J.R. Simplot. The Simplot plant sits just outside of the reservation and clearly falls within the jurisdiction of the state and county who have regulated it for years. The Astaris facility sits just inside reservation boundaries on privately owned land. Jurisdictional disputes over who should regulate Astaris resulted in a stalemate while the plant continued to pollute the environment. Essentially, FMC and the state of Idaho felt that the Fort Hall Shoshone- Bannock Indian Tribes did not have jurisdiction, technical expertise, financial resources, or regulatory enforcement capability. This situation and the attitudes it revealed led to poor relations between the state and the tribe—hence the cancellation of the MOA.[10] Finally, the EPA stepped in and fined the owners $12 million in 1998. While the tribes and the state were battling over jurisdiction, the area around the plant was becoming one of the most contaminated sites in the country and was having an adverse impact on both state and tribal air and water.[11] This example underscores one of the problems that Roger Turner sees as plaguing relations between most tribes and states—jurisdictional confusion. He feels that land issues need to be clarified by federal statute so that *Indian country, trust land,* and other key terms are defined. In his words,

Where things get fuzzy across the country is when there are privately held lands within reservation borders or when the tribe owns land outside of the boundaries that they are trying to put in trust. Those areas are where the state has the greatest problem with tribes asserting their authority.[12]

Even with the jurisdictional problems that hamper state-tribal cooperation in Idaho (in the area of air quality management), by and large, the relations between the state and the tribes have improved in recent years, with any problems stemming from jurisdictional issues and the exercise of those rights rather than any environmental issues. Thus there may be hope that the environment, rather than turf battles, becomes the driving force. While the Shoshone-Bannock tribes do not have an MOA with the state, Roger Turner is quick to point out that several tribes do have working MOAs with their respective states that are working well. In those cases the two sides have agreed to set aside jurisdictional differences in order to protect the environment. Turner is hopeful that the tribes and the state of Idaho can reach that point too.[13]

Water Quality Management

The Shoshone-Bannock tribes have their own water quality program and are in the process of having a set of water quality standards approved by the EPA. As for state-tribal cooperation in the area of water quality management, there are no formal agreements, but a Memorandum of Understanding (MOU) is currently in the negotiation stage. The area under discussion is narrowly focused and centers on monitoring TMDLs (total maximum daily loads), which is the current approach to monitoring the quality of a waterway.[14]

The MOU discussion has been going on since the summer of 2000 and negotiations really haven't gotten into any specifics.[15] There are a number of reasons for this, and it appears that finalizing any sort of formal agreement is a fairly low priority—for both sides. The tribal negotiators and water agency people feel the state doesn't always act as if they accept the tribes as equals. In other words, they are not really looking to negotiate from a true perspective of cooperation. Similarly, the tribe views the state with a certain amount of mistrust, and the tribal chairman is looking for some sort of MOU that outlines specifically what is expected of each side and what each side can and cannot do.[16] The primary concern, it seems, is jurisdiction.

According to tribal attorney Janet Wolfley, there are more jurisdictional issues with water because of the large number of rivers and streams that go through the reservation or start there and then go off. The nature of the jurisdictional uncertainty is compounded by issues such as control of riverbeds, monitoring (whether the state can come onto the reservation to monitor), and water quality (especially for rivers that leave the reservation clean and then re-enter polluted).

Fortunately, the tribe and state are now able to avoid another major hurdle to effective tribal-state cooperation that plagues many tribes and states in the West—the antagonism surrounding water quantification. It is inevitable that quantity comes first and quality comes after. When working on quality, it is still water. People hear the word *water* and they think quantity and then tend to back off. This is something that has become ingrained in the minds of most people out west. Fortunately the tribe has had on-reservation water rights quantified so that attention can now turn to quality—if they can overcome differences with jurisdictional issues.

When asked what would be necessary for the state and tribe to move forward with future negotiations on water-related issues, the tribal attorney had three primary suggestions. The first was that both sides needed to put aside petty squabbles over jurisdiction so that they could focus on fixing the problem at hand. In her words, "We can always argue about jurisdiction, but if the people at the table can say 'we agree to disagree about that,' we can work toward the bigger issue of the environment."[17] She also suggested that the discussion needs to remain focused on a single issue. For example, if they only talk about TMDL monitoring, their chances of reaching an agreement are much better than if they are also discussing streambeds or fishing rights. Finally, the discussion needs to be driven, at least initially, by technical people.[18] Those in the trenches are the most knowledgeable about how a program should be run, what the technical requirements would be for each side, and how each side could be best utilized. There is also the tendency for these people to care more about the environment than territory. The same can be true for social workers, air quality technicians, water quality technicians, or law enforcement officers—those in the trenches tend to share a core set of beliefs about what it is that they do. This core set of beliefs can lead to the mutual respect that is needed for cooperation and effective negotiation. Once these people have had a chance to fully work things out, then it is time to bring in the higher level, political leaders and present them with a full working agreement that is backed up by facts and technical expertise.

Law Enforcement

The relationship between the Fort Hall Tribal Police and the state and surrounding counties can be best summed up through the words of a Fort Hall officer who declares that, "Officers on the road work well together—when the problems come in, it's elected officials. They don't always get along all of the time."[19] As a PL 280 state, there are certain areas where the tribe does not have police authority. This leads to some jurisdictional problems and a number of issues on which the tribal council and the county sheriff do not see eye to eye. Most of the problems with jurisdictional conflict come from the county and not the state.

Not all counties are the same, and the relationships with various counties and county sheriffs differ. Since the Fort Hall Reservation is touched by Bannock, Bingham, Caribou, and Power Counties, we can see that there is not a one-size-fits-all approach to understanding state-tribal or county-tribal relations. While the constants in this particular setting are the Shoshone-Bannock tribes, we find that the relations change by county. Many of the surrounding areas recognize tribal jurisdiction but would take over if they could. These counties do not like having their authority limited. One county, however, is different—at least in the way they deal with the tribe. There is a working MOU between the tribal police and Power County that provides for joint law enforcement and attempts to smooth out jurisdictional differences. In this MOU, the county and tribe have both given respect to the other's jurisdiction and have formally addressed what each side can and cannot do—it also addresses ways in which the two agencies can assist one another without stepping over jurisdictional bounds. Thus far, the agreement "has worked pretty well."[20] The question is why there is a MOU with Power County and not with Bannock, Bingham, and Caribou Counties. Part of the answer is simply disagreement over the goals of the agencies and over the ever-present question of jurisdiction. The disagreement, however, stems from a more complex set of circumstances. Political posturing and the intricacies of PL 280 in Idaho cause the disagreement. PL 280 raises a number of questions, and citizens on both sides really do not understand what it is and what its ramifications really are. For example, many tribal members do not understand that the state and county have jurisdiction over state and county roads that run through the reservation. When they see a non-tribal officer on the reservation, they feel it is an invasion—a violation of sovereign rights—and they call a council member. The council member (who is equally undereducated on all of PL 280's implications) places a call to the tribal police to have them remedy the situation. The tribal police are then seen as being ineffective because they aren't keeping the invaders out. Politically, the council wants full jurisdiction—legally they do not have it.[21] The same happens for the county sheriff's department—the county board wonders why certain areas on the reservation are not policed according to state or county law. They, like the tribal council, must respond to a constituency that may desire full authority without realizing they do not legally have it. The only people that suffer from such a situation are the officers on the street (who tend to get along fine) and the citizenry on both sides of the border who do not have the law enforcement that they could have.

Some states and tribes have worked toward maximizing resources and making the overall law enforcement scheme more effective through formal cross-deputization. This is not likely to happen in Idaho unless there is some retro cession of PL 280 that will give the tribes full authority within reservation borders. The Shoshone-Bannock tribes have been working on such retro cession, but it is a slow process. Until then, the best that they can hope for is the MOU approach that they have with Power County. If the surrounding areas see that this works, perhaps they might be willing to forgo the jurisdictional squabbles and focus on the larger issue—public safety.

Other Issues

Hunting and Fishing

The major issue that divides the Shoshone-Bannock Tribes and the state of Idaho with regard to game and fish is whether the Fort Bridger Treaty of 1868 allows tribal members to hunt off of the reservation without a state permit. The state has repeatedly said no, while the tribe has said yes. The matter goes beyond the question of wildlife management—it strikes at the strength of the treaty rights granted to the tribe. In determining who is right, battle lines are being drawn. Between 1995 and 1997 alone there were five Shoshone-Bannock tribal members cited in three separate incidents.[22]

In an attempt to resolve the issue, a group of Shoshone-Bannock met with several state legislators and agents for the Idaho Department of Fish and Game. The meeting was requested by State Senator Bob Lee, who had hoped to stop the name calling and political fallout that was coming from non-natives who felt they were not being allowed to hunt in the same manner as the Shoshone-Bannock. That the non-natives were never force marched from their homes and asked to sign an agreement relinquishing title to their land as payment for the right to hunt did not matter. The general public was outraged and was exerting political pressure on both the state legislature and, in turn, the Idaho Department of Fish and Game. At the meeting the tribe insisted that this was one right that was non-negotiable—it was treaty granted. Representatives from the state claimed that they were not seeking to change treaty rights, but were looking for a way to cooperatively diffuse the situation. To the tribe, "cooperatively" meant doing what the state wanted. According to a tribal official, "They told us what they want, not what we want."[23] Regardless of their different perspectives, both sides acknowledged that there was not much cooperation at the meeting. The result is that the state and tribe will rely on the time tested (and from a cooperative perspective, time failed) litigation approach.

General Climate

The lack of widespread cooperative efforts in law enforcement and environmental management can possibly be explained by what appears to be a generally hostile attitude toward Indians in Idaho. In a similar vein, the tribal council is fiercely isolationist and protective of sovereignty—even in what might appear to be minor instances such as a tribal leader pushing for trespassing citations against county officers who stray from state roads (where they do have jurisdiction).[24] The tribe is also flexing its muscle, and alienating a potentially powerful ally, by requiring reporters who come onto the reservation to purchase a business license. The tribe is emphasizing its sovereign right by enforcing a 1992 tribal law that requires any organization doing business on the reservation to purchase an annual business license for $150. The news media is outraged and feels that this violates their First Amendment rights. While the $150 would not be a financial burden, most area radio and news sources have refused to pay.[25] They will certainly not stop reporting on the tribe, but will be forced to get their information elsewhere—something that may not improve on the general misconceptions that often drive state-tribal relations.

The state is not without blame in the creation of a generally tense atmosphere. The issue of gaming has been a hot topic and a source of conflict for quite some time. In early 2001, the Idaho Senate killed a bill that would have allowed tribes to increase their number of slot machines. Since the issue was not resolved either through the compacting process, which would have been the most favorable approach from a cooperative standpoint, or through state legislation, the issue will have to go through the federal court system.[26] The issue will drag on for several more years and will remain a source of tension between the state and tribes.

Another source of tension is the perception that the state perpetuates stereotypes, allows for racism on official state landmarks, and is generally insensitive to the feelings of American Indians. The latest incident involves the use of the term "squaw," which is actually a derogatory term that refers to female genitalia. The members of the House State Affairs Committee who voted against removing the term from state sites disagreed, and stated that the term simply refers to an Indian woman. Who gets to decide? The legislature. What is at stake? Long-term relations with the tribe. Given that the House vote was met with cries such as "the 'S-word' is a historical sexual harassment of women" and "unfortunately the state of Idaho is still a state of hate," it is clear that this was a salient issue to a number of people.[27] If these people were upset enough to protest at the state capitol, they are certainly upset enough to protest back on the reservation when the state and tribe sit down to discuss other issues. Trust and respect are easy to destroy and hard to rebuild.

SUMMARY AND KEY POINTS

There is a generally tense relationship between the tribes and the state of Idaho, and both sides share responsibility. At the core is a general feeling of mistrust and misunderstanding that makes everyone involved approach issues in a very tentative manner. There is no respect, and until bridges are built, widespread cooperation will not occur. There are glimmers of hope, and relations have improved over time. The water quality people are trying to negotiate a working MOU, and law enforcement officials have been able to forge an active agreement with Power County.

There are a number of reasons why some agencies are able to move forward while others are not. Looking at the relationship between the Shoshone-Bannock Tribes, the state of Idaho, and the surrounding counties, we find that the following are possible solutions to the jurisdictional stalemate that plagues the overall state-tribal relationship:

1. Sovereignty and a true willingness to treat each other as equals—Sovereignty is the lifeblood of both state and tribal existence. If true cooperation is ever to occur, sovereignty must be respected and maintained. A major hurdle for the state and tribes in their environmental negotiations is the perception that the tribe is not being viewed as an equal—as a sovereign. For true cooperation to occur, a partnership must be formed. Until the state can concede sovereignty and technical ability, cooperation will not occur. The face-to-face discussions that have been successful in other cases appear to be missing here. If the two sides would sit down and listen to what the other has to offer, perhaps they would find common ground and some of the misconceptions could dissipate.

2. Focus on issue and let technocrats start—A suggestion was that negotiations should start with the technocrats rather than the higher level administrators. This suggestion has been made in other cases, and certainly makes sense—especially with the perception that the tribe is being discounted. If the lower level, technical, people meet first, they may find that their goals and mission are essentially the same—the protection of the environment, the community, etc. These people are more likely to forego jurisdictional differences, focus on the common cause, and develop a framework for cooperation. Moreover, if the technical people find that there is an equal level of knowledge and expertise, and that both sides could benefit from a *mutual* relationship, this information could be passed upward. Despite political pressure on the politicos, strong technical support and information can sway decisions.

3. Clarification of land status—The Shoshone-Bannock and the state of Idaho seem to be no different here than any of the other cases. Despite having only 4 percent of their land in fee status, even a small blending of fee and trust property leads to the possibility of jurisdictional confusion and political posturing. The ability to question jurisdiction gets in the way of bringing two sides together. Moreover, these differences are generally resolved in court—an adversarial process that further separates the two governments. It may be a utopian ideal, but the consensus is that universal clarification of land status might be an important step in forging state-tribal relations.

4. Education—Misconceptions about land status, tribal conditions, state jurisdiction (PL 280), the term "squaw," and other issues all stem from a lack of education. People are being driven by a bounded rationality that precludes meaningful discussion. Both the state and tribe are guilty. Both are political bodies being pressured by constituencies—constituencies that perpetuate a bias against one another based on limited knowledge and fear of the uncertain.

NOTES

1. "Historic Fort Hall," http://www.sho-ban.com/history.htm.
2. U.S. Department of Commerce, *American Indian Reservation.*

3. http://www.nps.gov/ciro/cultural.htm.
4. U.S. Department of Commerce, *American Indian Reservation*.
5. Ibid.
6. Ibid.
7. F. Farsi, *Summary Information on the Shoshone-Bannock Tribes*. Land Use Department, Fort Hall, Idaho, March 1995.
8. Roger Turner, interview by Jeff Ashley, telephone interview, June 2002, on file with author.
9. Ibid.
10. F. Farsi, interview by Secody Hubbard, personal interview, March 1995.
11. Josh Manning, "Sho-Ban Tribes, Astaris Reach Agreement on Wastewater Facility," *Idaho Falls Post Register*, 23 February 2001.
12. Turner, interview.
13. Ibid.
14. Janet Wolfley, interview by Jeff Ashley, telephone interview, May 2002, on file with author.
15. Elise Teton, interview by Jeff Ashley, telephone interview, May 2002, on file with author.
16. Ibid.
17. Wolfley, interview.
18. Ibid.
19. Captain Torrey Trahant, interview by Jeff Ashley, telephone interview, June 2002, on file with author.
20. Ibid.
21. Ibid.
22. See Warren Cornwall, "Tribes Claim Hunting Rights on State Lands," *Idaho Falls Post Register*, 24 December 1997; Dan Egan, "Tribe Tests Treaty Laws on Hunting," *Idaho Falls Post Register*, 26 March 1995; and Brandon Loomis, "Indian Hunting Rights to Be Subject of Trials," *Idaho Falls Post Register*, 31 December 1996.
23. Gene Fadness and Lucille Edmo, "Tribe Refuses to Relinquish Hunting Rights," *Idaho Falls Post Register*, 20 December 1996.
24. "Shoshone-Bannocks Could Cite Local Police on Reservation Land," Associated Press State and Local Wire, 25 October 2001.
25. Matthew Evans, "Sho-Ban to Charge Media to Report on Tribal Land," *Idaho Falls Post Register*, 4 January 2002.
26. Bob Flick, "Idaho Senate Kills Bill that Promotes Tribal Slots," *Deseret News*, 27 March 2001.
27. Corey Taule, "Protestors of 'Squaw' Get No Answers from Kempthorne," *Idaho Falls Post Register*, 10 March 2001.

CHAPTER 9

The St. Regis Mohawk Nation

The presence of the Mohawk people in the Northeast predates the colonial period and the creation of the state of New York by at least 500 years. The Mohawk Nation is one of five founding nations of the Iroquois Confederacy, which was formed sometime between 1000 and 1450—well before the arrival of the Europeans. The true name of these long-term residents is KANIEN'KEHAKE or "People of the Flint." The name "Mohawk" was given to them by the Algonquin Nation and was later adopted by the British, Dutch, French, and Americans because it was easier to spell and to pronounce. While Mohawk is not their true name, most tribal members have come to accept the term in the same manner as they have grudgingly accepted the term "Indian"—it has been used by others for so long that it is simply easier to go along.[1]

The region that was inhabited by the People of the Flint was Akwesasne. While they were generally nomadic, Akwesasne was one area that they returned to year after year. In this sense, Akwesasne was an established settlement with a large population long before 1752, when a group led by the Reverend A. Gordon arrived from down river to establish a mission. The project took quite some time and was actually completed in 1789 by the Reverend J.A. McDonnell and his followers. They named the mission St. Regis after St. Jean Francis Regis, who had wanted to work among the Indians. St. Regis never made it to the new territory to work with the native people, but he did make numerous financial contributions that later led to the St. Regis Mission being named after him.[2] Those Mohawk located in the part of Akwesasne immediately surrounding the mission became known as the St. Regis Mohawk Tribe.

The St. Regis Mohawk split with the majority of the Seven Nations Confederacy by siding with the colonists during the Revolutionary War. All of the tribes were treated similarly, however, when the war was over and attention turned toward other matters. One of the matters was how to deal with Indians in the newly acquired nation. In 1796, New York entered into The Seven Nations of Canada Treaty, which granted over six square miles (and other smaller collateral tracts) of land to the tribes in return for the promise that no further land claims would be made against the state in the future. The state also agreed to pay annuities to each of the tribes under separate negotiated agreements. This agreement was modified by the state in the mid-1830s when it decided that it would only pay money to those tribes residing on the New York side of the reservation (a portion of the Indian reserve falls in Canada).[3]

The St. Regis Mohawk Indian Reservation is located in the northernmost part of the state of New York and is bisected by the U.S./Canada border. The territory on which the reservation is located, called Akwesasne, is divided into two separate jurisdictions. The southern part of Akwesasne territory lies within the United States and is home to approximately 8,000 St. Regis Mohawk people. The land base of this portion of the reservation has a total of 14,640 acres, all tribal-owned.

Due to its location and history, there are actually three separate government bodies within the territory of Akwesasne. The Mohawk National Council is the oldest and the one closest to the traditional form of government recognized by the Mohawk people for generations. The Mohawk National Council views all of the lands of Akwesasne as being one geopolitical territory—in other words it chooses to ignore the obvious separation in territory imposed by the U.S./Canada border.

The St. Regis Mohawk Tribal Council is recognized as the "official" tribal government for the St. Regis Mohawk Tribe. The Tribal Council was created in 1802 by the New York legislature and originally consisted of three "trustees" and a "clerk." This group represented the interests of the people and also interacted with the state of New York and the United States. Although the Mohawk people kept their traditional ways, the strong non-native influence on the structure of the tribal government encouraged the original designated trustees to evolve into the present form of government, the Tribal Council. The Tribal Council consists of three chiefs and three sub-chiefs. Each is elected at large by tribal membership and each serves three-year staggered terms. The tribal council chiefs are not only responsible for setting overall policy and making decisions on behalf of the tribe, but also oversee the day-to-day internal administrative operation of the tribal government.

The third Mohawk government is the Mohawk Council, which was created by the Canadian legislature and the Department of Indian Affairs in 1899.[4] Based on the location of their creating bodies, the St. Regis Mohawk Tribal Council views its area of political authority as those tribal lands south of the U.S./Canada border, while the Mohawk Council views their area of jurisdiction as being the lands north of the border. Similarly, New York and the United States Bureau of Indian Affairs views the St. Regis Mohawk Tribal Council as the recognized government in the United States and the Canadian government looks to the Mohawk Council of Akwesasne as being the legitimate representative of the Mohawk community north of the border. The Mohawk Nation Council is not recognized by the state of New York, the United States, or Canada.[5]

Among the most often cited reasons for state-tribal conflict are jurisdictional disputes and differing goals.[6] In the case of the St. Regis Mohawk, the jurisdictional confusion goes beyond that experienced by most tribes, and the internal divisions appear to be greater as well. The United States and Canada assume jurisdiction over parts of the community of Akwesasne while New York and the provinces of Ontario and Quebec assume jurisdiction within parts of the same area. Added to this are the three internal governments—the Mohawk National Council, the Mohawk Council, and the St. Regis Mohawk Tribal Council. This results in eight governmental entities assuming jurisdiction over segments of this small patch of land.[7]

To add to this complex governmental arrangement, additional political fracturing would plague the Mohawk Nation and add to the obstacles standing in the way of greater tribal-state cooperation. First, in the late 1980s, a strong push came from more traditional forces within the tribe who created a group within the nation called the Warrior Society. Second, a major division occurred within the St. Regis Mohawk Tribal Council (the recognized government that deals with the state of New York). This division resulted in two sets of chiefs—one set called The Peoples' Government and the other the Constitutional Government. Obviously, there are different goals emanating out of each one of these two groups. Finally, New York initiated the process of repealing the 1802 legislation that created the St. Regis Tribal Council in the first place.[8] To say that confusion reigns and that tensions are high would be an understatement. This provides the backdrop for examining the various policy areas currently being navigated by the tribe and the state as we look for ways to forge greater cooperation between the two.

STATE-TRIBAL RELATIONS

Environmental Management

Air Quality Management

Tribal Air Quality Management is one of the many programs operated by the St. Regis Mohawk Environment Division. Some of these programs include Soil Analysis, Solid Waste Management, a Clean Water Program under the Clean Water Act, and a Water Purification Project. Although the air quality program is still relatively young (it began in 1990) there have been vast improvements in tribal air management, such as setting tribal air quality standards, monitoring and testing, source identification, and cooperation with the state and private industries adjacent to the reservation.

The development of the Clean Air Program began with an inventory of non-point sources on and near the reservation. The program also included international sources of air pollutants, as the reservation is bisected by the U.S./Canada border. Sources were identified by name, emissions type, rates, and annual amount. During the second grant year in 1991, the staff continued to obtain emission source information and began training personnel with the Air Pollution Training Institute (APTI) of the EPA. The staff further developed intergovernmental ties with the state of New York and the EPA's Region II Department of Environmental Conservation and Health. During the third and fourth year, training and development were continually emphasized, along with establishing concrete ties with the state of New York Department of Environmental Conservation (NYDEC). Additionally, the tribe began air toxic sampling and developed two air monitoring stations and a meteorological station. Today the Mohawk Air Quality Program has intensive sampling plans and monitoring efforts for polyaromatic hydrocarbons (PAHS), volatile organic compounds (VOCS), fluoride, petroleum hydrocarbons, and other airborne contaminants. Training of personnel and the operation of the weather and air monitoring stations are carried out on a continual basis.

Cooperation between the state and tribe is now mostly informal and based on mutual understanding in the spirit of partnership. Informal cooperation is preferred at a management-to-management level because personnel having the same technical and professional background can meet face-to-face and understand the problems and issues facing their respective organizations. Tribal personnel also feel that informal interorganizational cooperation does not take on a political character, whereas formal agreements have to be reviewed by tribal staff attorneys and the chief elected official. The process of legal review and breaking through both the state and tribal bureaucracy is time consuming and delays program implementation. Thus a de-politicized process is preferred. The state and tribe have, however, worked out several formal agreements for specific areas—one that bears mention is a vegetation fluoride sampling plan.[9]

The sampling plan came about through over a dozen face-to-face meetings between the tribe, the state, and private industry. By meeting face-to-face, all of the parties were able to find out what one another had in terms of goals and interests. They were also able to identify any miscommunications or misconceptions that needed to be ironed out before the process could move forward. What really seemed to be a key ingredient to the success of this negotiation, however, was the presence of an administrative law judge (ALJ) who served as a mediator. The state of New York had decided to experiment with this approach and asked the tribe if they wanted to participate—they did. With a neutral third party in place, everyone was able to build upon commonalities and set aside differences because whenever they got off track, the ALJ would bring them back. Outside issues such as land claims, taxation, and other areas of disagreement were kept out of the discussion so that the only thing being discussed was the sampling program. According to tribal air quality manager Les Benedict, "We have land claims issues, we have gaming issues which are very important to us, but anytime that they are brought into an issue like the air, the only thing that would happen is that you won't be able to accomplish anything and will just spin your wheels. In this case we had the good fortune of having an administrative law judge act as a mediator."[10] It is clear that having a third party in place was critical. Prior to this, no formal air quality agreements between the state and tribe were in place.

Water Quality Management

The St. Regis Mohawk tribe has developed its own set of water quality standards and is waiting for EPA approval. While the standards are very similar to those of the state, it has taken the EPA over two years to review the standards and enforcement plan because of ongoing land claims issues between the tribe and state. In the interim, the tribe is working directly with the EPA on a government to government basis. While the one-on-one approach is partly driven by the tribes-as-states movement, the Mohawk Tribal Council is not particularly fond of the wording "tribes-as-states." They do not wish to be considered a state because they feel that tribes hold a higher status than states—a feeling that tends to get in the way of state-tribal cooperation.[11]

The biggest problem facing the St. Regis Mohawk water supply is a toxic landfill created by waste disposal from a General Motors foundry near the reservation. During the 1950s Reynolds Metals, ALCOA, and GM all had plants that were polluting the St. Lawrence River. By 1975, those living on the reservation were noticing the effects—farmers were seeing an increased rate of stillborn cattle, fish that were an important part of the culture began to dwindle, and children at a school near the GM plant were getting sick and complaining of headaches. The problem was PCB contamination.[12]

It has become so bad that some turtles in Turtle Cove have ingested enough PCBs that the animals themselves are considered toxic waste—moving waste sites. This is a rather sad reflection of the changing Mohawk existence, as tribal folklore has it that the world was created on the back of a turtle. Finally, in 1983, the EPA placed the GM site on the Superfund priority list as one of the nation's worst toxic waste sites. Despite some improvement, the EPA is learning that the site is more contaminated than they ever imagined. Still, the EPA is giving GM credit for making progress while the tribe (and apparently state) is angry. It has been close to thirty years since symptoms of PCB exposure were noticed and roughly twenty years since the EPA designated the dump as a Superfund site. In an unusual move, the state and tribe announced that they would join forces to sue GM for violating New York's environmental laws. The assistant attorney general assigned to the case announced that this was a blatant case of environmental racism and that GM was dragging its feet because the Mohawk were a relatively poor, voiceless group of people. He said,

this is another example of a Native American community being treated as second-class citizens. I guarantee you if this site was located next to a very middle-class, white neighborhood, this site would be well on its way to being remediated.[13]

It looked like the state and tribe were on their way to formalizing a cooperative effort (the lawsuit) when suddenly the attorney general pulled out, saying that he wanted to see more negotiations between the tribe and General Motors. There are a number of explanations for the reversal—spillover from unsettled land claims and taxation issues (being handled by the attorney general's office), economic pressure from GM pushing the issue beyond an environmental concern to a larger political issue that the attorney general wanted no part of, or simply that there was a desire to avoid litigation and that more negotiation would be truly beneficial. Regardless of the reasons, the tribe was shocked at the change of position.[14] They were tired of talking to GM—they had been talking for thirty years—but needed the state's support for the suit. They were not, however, surprised—the tribe has grown accustomed to uncertainty when dealing with the state of New York and its various agencies and actors.

The manager of the Mohawk Water Program points out that the breakdown between the parties over the lawsuit is a great example of how decisions begin to break down once they get larger and more political. The assistant attorney general was eager to pursue the case—when it became a larger, more public issue, the attorney general dropped out. It also points to the fact that individuals and offices differ. One cannot paint the entire state of New York with the same brush. The Mohawk water people have good and bad relations depending upon the agency's particular institutional culture and the individuals within those agencies. It is clear the relations with the attorney general are not stellar, and they also have problems with the people in the Game and Fish Department. They do, however, have a positive, cooperative relationship with the Department of

Health (DOH). While there are no formal agreements in place (much like the informal arrangements with the air quality division), the tribe and the DOH routinely share information and technical expertise in the joint effort to improve and protect public health.[15]

Law Enforcement

Relations between the tribe and state in the area of law enforcement appear to be a mixture of camaraderie blended with politics and jurisdictional confusion. The officers working side by side have a positive working relationship and are quick to back one another up. Such support and back-up comes without being asked and tribal police and other street-level bureaucrats enjoy good rapport. According to one member of the tribal police, "It's friendship! They stop by and have coffee with us and we get along great.... We're in the same sandbox so we can't throw sand—everyone has to play nice."[16]

The mutual respect became a necessity when tribal police were stripped of arrest authority by the Franklin County Sheriff, Jack Pelkey, in 2000. Prior to this, the tribal police were allowed to arrest non-natives for infractions taking place on the reservation. Ironically, it was Pelkey who signed the agreement that allowed for the expanded power to begin with. Normally, tribal police have arrest authority over their own members but can only detain non-natives and put in a call to state, city, or county police officers to have them pick up the offender and charge them under state law. In order to make things more expedient and efficient, the sheriff's department had contracted with the tribal police and signed an agreement with the Tribal Council in 1995. Subsequent to this, the Constitutional Government took over—Pelkey signed a similar agreement with them in 1999. In 2000, the Constitutional Government was out, and the Tribal Council was back in.[17] Despite the change, the agreement might have remained intact if the relationship hadn't been strained by external political forces.

On Wednesday, March 1, 2000, the Mohawk Police set up a roadblock to stop two Canadian fuel trucks from delivering to several on-reservation businesses. The tribal police were operating under orders issued by the Tribal Council, who asserted that the businesses owed the tribe over $200,000 in licensing fees and unpaid fines.

Since the tribal police were operating under a contract with the county, the sheriff felt that the officers should have followed his orders, which were to let the trucks through. He had been informed by county officials that stopping the trucks could result in a lawsuit against the county. In this case, the two law enforcement bodies were being pulled apart by elected officials. The Tribal Council was pulling the tribal police in one direction and the county board was pulling the sheriff in the other. As a result of the roadblock, the state police were forced to come onto the reservation and patrol the area for a time.[18] The fiasco was very visible and political. According to Chief Andrew Thomas of the Mohawk Police, "The sheriff's hands were tied."[19] Tribal arrest authority was removed the next day and has not been restored.

The lack of arrest authority has led to a number of problems, and both the tribe and sheriff's department tend to be rather guarded when discussing the issue. The primary concern is to avoid another huge political standoff between the tribe and county in which the street level officers get caught in the middle. They depend upon one another for backup and need a positive working relationship.

The biggest problem with only having the authority to detain a suspect is that the tribal police cannot follow a case through to its final resolution. Even though harm may have come to a tribal member, once the case is turned over to the state or county the tribal police are out of the loop. Information on most cases cannot be legally shared, so the tribal police cannot keep the victim (the tribal member) apprised of any recourse. This can undermine the authority of the tribal police in the eyes of their own people. Under current law, however, there is not much that can be done unless tribal arrest authority is granted at the state level—something the tribal police are actively seeking.[20]

Other Issues

Taxation

The issue of taxation is a major source of tension between states and tribes across the country, and the St. Regis Tribe and the state of New York are no exception. The major issues here are excise taxes for tobacco and gasoline and the mechanism for tax collection. During the early 1990s Indian smoke shops and gas stations were becoming a solid core of tribal economic development. While the tax on gasoline and cigarettes rose dramatically in the state, the tribal operations were able to keep their prices lower by not requiring their customers to pay the higher taxes. It gave them a competitive advantage that surrounding businesses did not appreciate and it cost the state quite a bit in lost tax revenue. Even though the law actually required the collection of state taxes for non-Indian customers, St. Regis Mohawk operations thrived, in part, because they didn't make the distinction between tribal member and non-member—nobody paid the higher state tax. To rectify the situation, the state came up with a plan for tax collection that was challenged in court as a violation of treaty/sovereignty rights. In 1994, the U.S. Supreme Court upheld the plan. The tribes affected were not willingly abiding by the rule, however, continuing to assert that they never surrendered to the state and that they would only deal with the federal government—state taxation was a blatant violation of sovereignty. In 1995, the state actually planned for a military-like invasion into Mohawk, Onondaga, and Seneca reservations in order to collect the taxes. The plan—called Operation Gallant Piper—would have sent thousands of state troopers and national guard onto the reservations and would have been a costly, drastic move. Gallant Piper was officially canceled in February 1996, but the tax issue was still unresolved.[21]

In early May 1997 the state signed tentative agreements with several tribes that required them to impose cigarette and gasoline taxes on nonnatives. Four tribes did not sign and the St. Regis Mohawk was one of them. Many felt that the agreement was not a negotiated settlement, but an ultimatum. They pointed to the previously planned Operation Gallant Piper, with one opponent stating, "You can't negotiate with a figurative gun to your head."[22] News of the agreements spread, with state officials claiming that the Mohawk were part of the deal and the Mohawk claiming otherwise.[23] The state then planned a blockade of gas and tobacco shipments to the tribes who failed to sign the agreement—a move that intensified the resistance and made tensions run higher. One member of the protesting Mohawk stated, "Nobody's going to take my sovereignty, and nobody's going to take my kid's sovereignty. I'll stand up for it to all ends, whatever that may be."[24] Lines were being drawn, and people were prepared for battle. At the urging of a State Supreme Court justice, Governor Pataki announced that the state was abandoning its efforts to collect the taxes. When the announcement came on May 23, 1997, it was met with criticism by surrounding businesses and their respective political leaders and with cheers by the tribes who had successfully fought the state for their sovereign rights.[25] The ongoing nature of this issue and the intense antagonism it engendered cannot have helped future efforts for reaching cooperative agreements in other areas.

Land Claims/Gaming

Land has always been a contentious issue among the tribes, the states, and the federal government. As we have seen with tribes across the country, land promised through treaties has been dramatically reduced in many cases, and some areas are subject to dispute. One long-standing area of dispute is between the state of New York and several tribes. The Mohawk dispute actually covers the smallest amount of land—roughly 15,000 acres in Franklin and St. Lawrence Counties. The tribe filed suit against the state in a federal court alleging that the state illegally took treaty-provided reservation land. The dispute has been raging for decades and the lawsuit has been ongoing since 1982.[26]

In 1999 the state offered to pay the tribe $28 million plus $1 million a year for 50 years and also offered to provide the tribe title to portions of

Long and Croil Islands, but the tribe did not respond to the offer until 2001.[27] As of 2002, it appears that the tribe is viewing the initial proposal favorably as they look past the land claims issue toward a lucrative gaming compact. Plans have been under way for a large gaming operation, and the tribe has signed agreements with Nevada-based Park Place Entertainment to build the hotel-casino in the Catskills.[28] The tribe has even signed agreements with Sullivan County officials spelling out how much money the tribe would transfer to the county should a casino be built there. However, several legislators had pointed out that any land claim issues had to be resolved before any talks about the gaming compact with the state could occur. In this sense, the state was using the compact process as leverage in the land claims disputes—the dollar amount of the proposed St. Regis Mohawk settlement is far lower than what other tribes are seeking.[29] However, with the long-term potential returns from the casino, the tribe was willing to move forward. With the land dispute close to resolution, other areas may progress as well—gaming compacts and the long-awaited water quality standards from the EPA. The land claim will be one less source of tension, but it is too early to tell whether the use of gaming as a bargaining chip by the state will help to smooth future relations or will be viewed as blackmail and will make matters worse.

SUMMARY AND KEY POINTS

In the case of the St. Regis Mohawk Tribe and the state of New York, relations are clearly mixed. There has been some movement between the state and tribe to resolve long-standing land claims issues, but the negotiation also involved using gaming as leverage. The taxation issue seems to be resolved for the moment, but this is far from certain. While the state backed off, it is still theoretically able to collect taxes from non-natives generated on the reservation. As the state of the economy continues to deteriorate and the state looks for ways to plug holes in the budget, many may turn to the reservations once again. As for air and water quality management, there are some instances of successful cooperation and formal agreements such as the vegetation fluoride sampling plan, and some failed efforts, such as the proposed joint lawsuit against GM that never happened. There is also the issue of granted and rescinded arrest authority for tribal police and the obvious outcomes of that move. However, from the mixed relations experienced by the St. Regis Mohawk Tribe in the state of New York we can point to several obstacles that hinder cooperation and to some of the conditions that led to positive outcomes in the pursuit of greater tribal-state cooperation.

The following appear to be important areas for future negotiations:

1. Focus on the issue at hand—If possible, keep the topic narrow. Les Benedict made this very clear when discussing the successful negotiations over the veg-

etation fluoride sampling plan. He indicated that if other issues of contention were to enter into the debate, they would have gone nowhere. They were also successful because they were able to keep the topic narrow—vegetation sampling. The tribe really wanted animal testing as well, but the other parties weren't as interested and too much attention in that area would have hampered progress in the vegetation agreement.

2. Face-to-Face communication—For the air quality plan to happen, all of the parties had to meet face-to-face over a dozen times. Such talks were necessary to get all of the issues out in the open and to really determine where goals and priorities could be found. According to water quality manager Shawn Martin, the face-to-face communication is also necessary from an educational standpoint. Without such communication, neither side can really understand what programs and/or technical expertise the other has to offer. Since many tribes feel that they are perceived as being technologically inept, such an opportunity for education can be crucial. While the water quality people do not have formal agreements with the New York Department of Health, they do have effective communication and an understanding of what the other has to offer. The result is that the two agencies share information, advice, and expertise on a regular basis. Face-to-face communication appears to be helping with law enforcement as well. Despite the rescinded arrest authority, those working closest to one another—the officers on the street—have a good understanding of where the other is coming from and what they have to offer. They work cordially with one another and assist one another whenever possible. With the external pressure that pulled them apart, the face-to-face interaction has been crucial in reforming severed bonds.

3. Recognize sovereignty without political posturing—Both sides need to be aware of sovereign rights and mindful that both the state and tribe have goals and priorities that can differ. This is often done when the discussions begin at lower levels and then higher level, more political, actors are brought in. Often sovereignty and state rights are the driving force and become a focal point (thus a barrier) rather than something that can be worked out. Both sides have rights that need to be respected and preserved; however, both sides can also benefit from safe surroundings and a clean environment. Where possible, it may even be beneficial to remove jurisdictional boundaries, such as with air space or river systems, which have no boundaries. In an attempt to do this and to avoid the posturing, the air quality and water quality people from both the tribe and the state prefer to keep things informal and work with their counterparts on a technical level. They feel that cooperation is better and more gets accomplished when the politicians are kept at arm's length. There are times when an issue is inherently political or when discussions have reached a point where higher level actors need to sign off on a plan. Such was the case with the vegetation sampling plan—which was successful because it began at the technical level and all of the potential hurdles were ironed out before the tribal council or the governor were asked to become involved.

4. Make use of a third party—A particularly interesting aspect of the discussions held by the state and tribe is the positive response to making use of a third party. Both the state and tribe were pleased with the outcome of the experiment

with utilizing an administrative law judge for interagency negotiations. Many of the above mentioned obstacles, such as jurisdiction, multiple goals, posturing, education, face-to-face communication, and staying focused on a particular topic were all made less of a barrier to effective negotiation and cooperation because of mediation. Since many negotiations fall apart because of misconceptions and preconceived notions or positions, this approach may offer part of the solution for gaining more state-tribal cooperation in a wide range of areas.

NOTES

1. "Who Are the Mohawk?," http://www.peacetree.com/akwesasne/whoare.htm.

2. Ibid.

3. U.S. Department of Commerce, *American Indian Reservation*.

4. John Fadden, "Divisiveness at Akwesasne: Legacy of Nineteenth Century Colonialism" (1997) http://www.peacetree.com/akwesasne/division.htm.

5. Ibid.

6. Officials from the St. Regis Mohawk Tribe, Campo Band of Mission Indians, Navajo Nation, Shoshone-Bannock Tribe, Puyallup Tribe, and the Confederated Nation of the Salish and Kootenai, interviews by Jeff Ashley, telephone interviews, May 2002–August 2002, on file with author.

7. Fadden, "Divisiveness at Akwesasne."

8. Ibid.

9. Les Benedict, interview by Jeff Ashley, telephone interview, 31 May 2002, on file with author.

10. Ibid.

11. Shawn Martin, interview by Jeff Ashley, telephone interview, July 2002, on file with author.

12. Hart Seely, "Landfill Near Massena Polluting Water Where Mohawk Children Played," *Syracuse Herald American*, 24 June 2001.

13. Katie Thomas, "Toxic Threats to Tribal Lands," *Albany Bureau*, 25 March 2001.

14. S. Martin, interview.

15. Ibid.

16. Member of St. Regis Mohawk Tribal Police, interview by Jeff Ashley, telephone interview, June 2002, on file with author.

17. "Tribal Police Department Stripped of Authority after Road Block," Associated Press State and Local Wire, 3 March 2000.

18. Ibid.

19. Andrew Thomas, interview by Jeff Ashley, telephone interview, June 2002, on file with author.

20. Ibid.

21. Wilkins, *American Indian Politics*, p. 5.

22. Deborah Barfield, "Indians Map Tax Fight: NY Sales-Tax Levy Plan Called Sovereign Assault," *Newsday*, Nassau and Suffolk edition, 16 April 1996.

23. See "Deal Lets Native Americans Buy Tax-Free Tobacco, Petroleum," *Times Union*, 20 May 1997; and "Mohawk Leaders Deny Accord in Tax Dispute," *New York Times*, 21 May 1997.

24. "Interstate Is Tied Up in Protest of Tax Deal," *New York Times*, 12 May 1997.

25. Wilkins, *American Indian Politics*, p. 6.

26. James Odato, "Tribe, State Discuss Settling Land Claim: Eyeing Casino Deal, Mohawks Upbeat about Resolving Lawsuit," *Times Union*, 25 August 2001.

27. James Odato, "Pataki Land Claim Tied to Casino," *Times Union*, 28 February 2002.

28. Mary Esch, "Gambling Promoters Explore NY Casinos' Future at Gaming Summit," Associated Press State and Local Wire, 9 April 2002.

29. Odato, "Resolving Lawsuit."

PART III
Looking Forward

CHAPTER 10

Conclusion: New Directions for State-Tribal Relations

As we attempt to understand the complexity of the existing federal system and the historically tense relations between tribes and states, one point must be made abundantly clear—not all states and tribes are the same. They have different goals and different political climates. What holds true for the Navajo Nation and the state of Arizona may not be reflective of the relationship between Arizona and the White Mountain Apache Tribe or even the Mescalero Apache Tribe. In addition, as cultures and society evolve, the goals and desires of a people can change. Any description of a relationship can really be nothing more than a snapshot in time. Therefore, speculating broadly from six cases would be a tremendous mistake. However, the commonalities revealed with these six are so strong and so consistent that they must be telling us something about state-tribal relations. The common themes are broad enough that they can be generically applied to any state-tribal relationship in an attempt to foster greater understanding and cooperation. Before looking at the tactics that can be used for building new traditions, we will look at two major hurdles that are remnants of the past. These are roadblocks that are constantly getting in the way of positive relations. The only way to eventually avoid them is to recognize them as obstacles and move on.

THE CHECKERBOARD

One area that is universally discussed as serving to hinder states and tribes in their attempts to cooperate and negotiate is the uncertainty over mixed areas containing trust and fee land. The so-called checkerboard is at the heart of many jurisdictional battles. Even when states and tribes have looked to one another and attempted to forge new bonds, some have recognized the checkerboard as a problem. For example, the governor of South Dakota brought tribes together in 1995 to usher in a new era of state-tribal cooperation. The governor proclaimed, "We can work together. If it's on the reservation, it's yours. If it's off the reservation, it's ours. If it's in the checkerboard areas, we have trouble."[1] The case by case and issue by issue approach to resolving conflict in the checkerboard areas creates both tension and uncertainty. The tension stems from and leads to the continuous stream of litigation required to resolve jurisdictional claims in these areas. The uncertainty is due to the lack of a universal rule for laying out jurisdiction in these areas. With uncertainty comes inaction. With tensions already high, it seems that many states and tribes are reluctant to even attempt a joint venture because they do not understand the jurisdictional issues and legal ramifications of working in these areas. Hence the statement, "we are in trouble."

The only way that the murky jurisdictional questions in these areas can be resolved once and for all would be federal legislation that specifies exactly who has jurisdiction under certain circumstances. Given the way that federal action has exacerbated the problem in the past (they created the checkerboarding), however, pushing for such a remedy might not be in the best interest of either the states or the tribes. That said, while putting an end to the uncertainty would make life easier for states and tribes, the checkerboard problem is likely to plague state and tribal relations for quite some time. It may be difficult, but many states and tribes have been able to set aside jurisdictional debates and forge cooperative relationships in the face of jurisdictional uncertainty. These relationships and agreements respect autonomy, preserve sovereignty, and make more effective use of both state and tribal resources.[2] Other governments can look to them as a model.

HISTORY

When asked about the biggest hurdle facing states and tribes in their pursuit of positive relationships and cooperative efforts, one tribal administrator responded that, "The historic relationship between the tribe and state will often be the biggest factor in the directions of the relationship. That's usually not a good starting point."[3] There have been any number of treaties that have been broken, lives that have been lost, and lands that have been taken from tribes, and there is not a lot of trust. In addition, the adversarial legal system of the United States has often pitted states and tribes against one another as they attempt to resolve conflict. Such a win-lose approach has never created positive relations between the states and tribes. More importantly, there has never been a foundation built upon trust—the necessary ingredient for long-term relationships. Rather than exhibiting that they are willing to work for the betterment of the common good, both sides are guilty of posturing and positioning themselves to gain some sort of an advantage over the other. This, of course, stems from an adversarial system and historically bad relations. Overcoming this history is not easy! Racism has not disappeared and fear of unknown cultures leads people to behave acrimoniously toward one another. However, recognizing that this is omnipresent will allow for states and tribes to address the history head on and hopefully work through the tension over time. "It can be contentious as hell, you just make your bridges slowly."[4]

In addition to driving individual behavior, history has guided the actions of institutions. Bureaucratic agencies in particular have a tendency to establish standard operating procedures and organizational cultures that are often hard to shatter. Barzelay has discussed "Breaking Through Bureaucracy," and a wide variety of scholars have lamented that the bureaucracy is slow to change.[5] If the traditional way of dealing with other entities is to fight over jurisdiction and avoid cooperation, that is going to be continued. Part of the problem facing better state-tribal cooperation is that the institutions charged with developing these ties are currently incapable of doing so or are simply unwilling to make the effort without some sort of legislative or tribal mandate. Even with such a directive, building cooperative bridges in the wake of years of tension will not be easy. A new model for approaching state-tribal cooperation is needed.

NEW DIRECTIONS

States and tribes use a variety of methods to resolve conflict, including cooperative agreements, negotiation, memoranda of agreement or understanding, and informal working relationships. Unfortunately, the most common by far is litigation. Tribal-state dispute resolution has traditionally depended on judicial and legislative remedies, which normally end up in a win/lose situation. This method is the most costly and time consuming, generally does little to actually resolve conflict, and rarely promotes a deeper understanding of the problems, needs, and concerns of the other party.[6] Litigation generally leads to more litigation and, therefore, more divisiveness.

In 1978, the Commission on Tribal-State Relations was formed to facilitate a more cooperative effort in governmental relations. The Commission published two reports: *Handbook on State-Tribal Relations* and *State-Tribal Agreements: A Comprehensive Study (1981)*. The first report essentially deplored the adversarial character of both the states and the tribes, emphasized the "limits of litigation," and advocated that state and tribal governments begin from a common set of issues.[7] The report also noted that not all the problems in state-tribal intergovernmental relations stem from national legislation. Much of the confrontation also stems from the perception held by the participants that they can "win" by getting Congress to enact legislation favorable to their cause. Therefore "both should abandon the view that the support of Congress is a prize to be captured, useful for forcing the government's views on the other."[8] In other words, the report called on states and tribes to make two fundamental changes in their approach. First they need to stop looking to Congress for a solution to *their* problems. Second, and perhaps more important for our purposes, they implored the tribes and states to stop viewing all of their problems in terms of win/lose solutions. The second Commission report showed how some intergovernmental issues can be resolved through cooperative agreements without imposing exclusive turf protection and without jurisdictional conflicts in areas such as law enforcement, social services, tax collection, and, in some instances, natural resources.

Similar to the Commission's report, Gover, Stetson, and Williams describe tribal-state negotiations based on several case studies in which both the tribes and states are reluctant to negotiate and differ on many issues yet are making an effort to come together in areas of common interest. Negotiations in such cases thus tend to be the favored forum in which to settle intergovernmental differences that affect the citizenry of both state and reservation.[9] In *Intergovernmental Conflict and Indian Water Rights: An Assessment of Negotiated Settlements,* McCool concluded that negotiated settlements are flexible and substantive agreements that meet the specific situation. He notes that they are more humane and bestow a sense of legitimacy on all participants involved.[10] According to Peter Sly, these agreements also promote greater sovereignty and governmental integrity. He concludes that "ultimate self-determination for both states and tribes may be best served by negotiations that can tailor an agreement to present and future existing needs without the costs, friction, and delay of litigation."[11]

Another option in improving state-tribal relations and promoting cooperation is the tribal-state compact process. David Wilkins, in *Reconsidering the Tribal State Compact Process,* argues that because of the non-adversarial binding character, low cost, and mutual respect that characterize the compact process, tribal and state governments should use this method, which is no more than an agreement to deal with a problem or concern that crosses state boundaries. The compact process neither enlarges nor diminishes the governmental powers of states or Indian tribes, it simply outlines a specific plan for allocating and sharing resources.[12]

It is clear that alternatives to litigation are being promoted and pushed by a number of scholars and policy analysts. From compacts to negotiated settlements and even to informal work agreements, the trend is to advocate for a more cooperative approach for states and tribes to follow when

Conclusion

resolving conflict. Unfortunately, those who are being asked to cooperate—the states and tribes—aren't really being told how. The result is that negotiations are few and far between. In a survey of tribal water quality done by the National Indian Policy Center (NIPC), Gover, Stetson, and Williams note that of the 114 tribes reporting, only 16 tribes indicated they actually executed agreements with state governments and participated in discussions with local and state officials.[13] While this study was conducted in 1994, the numbers have not increased dramatically in 2002. States and tribes are simply not being given enough in the way of suggestions and tactics that will help them forge positive relationships. From looking at our six cases, however, the following appear to be universal strategies or suggestions that can provide that needed direction:

- agreeing to disagree on the issue of jurisdiction
- meeting face-to-face
- beginning discussions with the technocrats
- keying in on the narrow topic at hand
- having an overall policy or framework for adopting cooperative approaches or entering into agreements
- making use of a third party

Agreeing to Disagree on the Issue of Jurisdiction

In order for any negotiations to begin, there may be times when both sides need to "agree to disagree" on the issue of jurisdiction—at least initially. While sovereignty needs to be preserved, whenever talks turn to jurisdiction, things become adversarial. As the negotiations move forward, and some commonalities are discovered, it will be easier to discuss jurisdiction. Waiting on the issue of jurisdiction is especially important in those relationships dealing with checkerboarded land ownership. In the cases where positive relations have been formed and joint management agreements have emerged, jurisdiction has not been the central topic. In these cases, despite avoiding jurisdictional debate, sovereignty was maintained and preserved through the very nature of government-to-government negotiation.

Meeting Face-to-Face

If the goal of negotiation is to form relationships and develop trust, face-to-face meetings are very important. Body language and facial expressions can reveal as much or more than simple words. Moreover, face-to-face discussions are more humane and allow for a more free exchange of ideas, goals, and visions. In those cases where the two sides never met, relations were generally cordial at best. Those people who met in person, however, felt like they were really able to explain what their program or department was all about. They came away from the meeting feeling like they were better understood and that misconceptions were put to rest. Any opportunity to strip away years of misconception and bias should be utilized—face-to-face meetings can be one such opportunity.

Beginning Discussions with the Technocrats

Some literature suggests that any government-to-government negotiations have to be conducted by the tribal chairman and governor.[14] Of course any formal, signed documents will need the approval of a chairman, governor, council, or legislature, but these people do not have to initiate the process, nor should they in all cases. Without exception, the law enforcement and environmental people we spoke to stated that cooperation (thus coming to terms on the fundamentals of an agreement) is much greater at the lower, technical levels, and that discussions tend to disintegrate when they become politicized.

People enter into a given profession for a reason, and these people tend to share a core set of values that transcend jurisdictions. Water quality people want to protect the water supply regardless of where it begins and ends. Similarly, law enforcement officers want to have a safe community. Even with cultural differences in place, these people can talk on a professional, technical level. Once the discussion begins, and common ground is discovered, a general approach can be recommended to those whose signatures are necessary. The higher level officials may need to iron out some of the details, but they will have something tangible to work with and won't start out from political positions—which tend to be centered on jurisdiction.

Keying in on the Narrow Topic at Hand

When possible, negotiations should focus on a single, narrow topic. This should be the one and only thing that those in the room discuss. A problem that often emerges in negotiation is that the people involved want to cover too much. Once one topic has been covered, it may be possible to move on to another. However, every attempt should be made to avoid bringing in sensitive issues that muddy the waters and derail the development of the issue at hand. Every state and tribe are going to have some areas that are contentious. If these are brought into the discussion of something reconcilable, nothing will be accomplished. Remember the words of the Salish negotiator who helped forge a successful intergovernmental law enforcement agreement between the Salish-Kootenai and other governments, "If we would have added water rights or any of the other stuff into this agreement, I don't think it would have gone."[15]

Having an Overall Policy or Framework for Entering into Agreements

In our studies we found that having a policy that encourages cooperation is helpful in bringing the technical people together. Often, these people are at the lower levels of the bureaucracy and are uncomfortable instigating contact without being given prior approval or without having some set of guidelines to follow when the discussions begin. In addition, a policy or directive that actually encourages discussion and cooperative efforts conveys the feeling of support for such efforts. Both tribal workers and state workers are much more likely to engage in cross-communication if they feel it is wanted, supported, and encouraged. They will feel even better if they are provided with a general set of instructions on how to proceed. This approach was mentioned by one of our respondents, and successfully implemented by Arizona and the Navajo Tribe.

Making Use of a Third Party

Suggestions such as face-to-face communication, having professionals talk to professionals, avoiding contentious issues, and the like are all based upon one central idea. This idea is that states and tribes really are not that far apart on many issues. Unfortunately misconceptions, bias, and politics get in the way of two sides coming together in any meaningful way. In two of our cases, we found that relations were improved with the assistance of a third party who was able to act as a mediator between the factious sides. Making use of a mediator or neutral third party can go a long way toward having two sides find common ground from which negotiations and relationships can emerge.

By no means should this be construed as the definitive list of methods that can be employed when states and tribes attempt to reach a compromise position. Nor should this be viewed as a panacea for overcoming years of tension, litigation, and bad blood. There is no quick fix for overcoming misconceptions and biases that have developed over time. However, if these methods are employed on a consistent basis, and trust is allowed to gradually develop, relations will not be hurt. The keys to forging relationships that will endure are time and patience. The relationships and trust will take time to grow. Patience will be needed to stay the course when the results are not instantaneous. Remember, adverse relations were created over time so more positive relations will also take time. If patience is not a part of the long-term plan, the states and tribes will undoubtedly end up back in court. Such a move would take them back to the beginning.

Alternative dispute resolution will lead to less time and money being spent on litigation and more energy being put into solving the problems that face our communities. Moreover, cooperative efforts can allow for a more effective allocation of scarce resources and more innovative ways of addressing some of the issues that are of common interest to tribes and surrounding governments—especially those issues that tend to respect no boundaries like pollution and crime. As states and tribes enter into a new millennium, let us hope that they can build a bridge from the past and create a new era of state-tribal relations that is based upon mutual respect, cooperation, and innovation. Such an era would be of benefit to us all.

NOTES

1. Candy Hamilton, "Governor Janklow Meets with Oglala Tribal Leaders," *News from Indian Country,* August 1995.

2. Susan Johnson et al., *Government to Government: Understanding State and Tribal Governments* (Washington, D.C.: National Conference of State Legislatures, 2000), p. 2. This handbook was prepared in conjunction with the National Congress of American Indians.

3. William Sullivan, interview by Jeff Ashley, telephone interview, July 2002, on file with author.

4. Ibid.

5. See Michael Barzelay and Babak Armajani, *Breaking through Bureaucracy* (Berkeley, CA: University of California Press, 1992); and James Q. Wilson, *Bureaucracy* (New York: Basic Books, 1989).

6. Reed and Zelio, *States and Tribes,* p. 10.

7. Commission on State-Tribal Relations, *Handbook on State-Tribal Relations,* p. 75.

8. Ibid., pp. 75–76.

9. C. B. Stetson, B. K. Gover, and S. M. Williams, *1994 Survey of Tribal Water Quality. The National Indian Policy,* Washington, D.C., September 1994.

10. Daniel McCool, "Intergovernmental Conflict and Indian Water Rights: An Assessment of Negotiated Settlements," *Publius: The Journal of Federalism* 23 (winter 1993), pp. 85–101.

11. Peter Sly, "Federalism and Self-Determination: State Goals in Indian Rights Disputes," *Land and Water Law Review,* vol. 27, no. 1 (1992), pp. 71–77.

12. David E. Wilkins, "Tribal-State Compact Process."

13. Gover, Stetson, and Williams, *1994 Survey,* p. 58.

14. Reed and Zelio, *States and Tribes,* p. 10.

15. Les Clairmont, interview.

Bibliography

Anderson, William. *Understanding Intergovernmental Relations in Review.* Minneapolis, MN: University of Minnesota Press, 1960.
Arizona Department of Environmental Quality. *ADEQ Tribal Government Policy,* no. 0003.001. Issued 4 February 1994 and amended 9 May 1997.
Ashley, Jeffrey S. and Karen Jarratt-Ziemski. "Superficiality and Bias: The (Mis)Treatment of Native Americans in American Government Textbooks." *American Indian Quarterly,* vol. 23 (fall 1999).
Barfield, Deborah. "Indians Map Tax Fight: NY Sales-Tax Levy Plan Called Sovereign Assault." *Newsday,* Nassau and Suffolk edition, 16 April 1996.
Barzelay, Michael and Babak Armajani. *Breaking through Bureaucracy.* Berkeley, CA: University of California Press, 1992.
Benke, Richard. "Navajo Tribe Wants Six Navajo-Majority House Districts." Associated Press State and Local Wire, 7 January 2002.
Burton, Lloyd. *American Indian Water Rights and the Limits of the Law.* Lawrence, KS: University Press of Kansas, 1991.
Campo Band of Mission Indians Environmental Policy Act of 1990 as Amended. December 1994.
Campo Indian Reservation Nonpoint Assessment Report. June 1993.
Campo Indian Reservation Tribal Water Quality Assessment Report. November 1994.
Canby, William C., Jr., *American Indian Law in a Nutshell.* St. Paul, MN: West Publishing Company, 1988.
Castaldo, John. "Campo Casino Has County Upset: Project 10 Times as Big as Before." *San Diego Union-Tribune,* 10 May 2001.
Champagne, Duane. *Native America: Portrait of the Peoples.* Washington, D.C.: Visible Ink Press, 1994.
Chapter Images: General Facts on the Navajo Chapters. May 1990.

Clutter, Stephen. "Smoke Shop Breaks Pact, Government Officials Fume." *Seattle Times*, 11 January 1996.
Cohen, Felix S. *The Handbook of Federal Indian Law.* 1942.
Commission on State-Tribal Relations. *Handbook on State-Tribal Relations.* Albuquerque, NM: American Indian Law Center, n.d.
Commission on State-Tribal Relations. *State-Tribal Agreements: A Comprehensive Study.* Albuquerque, NM: American Indian Law Center, 1981.
Cooperative Agreement between the Campo Environmental Protection Agency and the State of California. 10 December 1992.
Cornell, Stephen. *The Return of the Native: American Indian Political Resurgence.* New York: Oxford University Press, 1988.
Cornell, Stephen and Joseph P. Kalt. "Public Choice, Culture, and American Indian Economic Development." Harvard University, 1988: 21.
Cornwall, Warren. "Tribes Claim Hunting Rights on State Lands." *Idaho Falls Post Register,* 24 December 1997.
"Deal Lets Native Americans Buy Tax-Free Tobacco, Petroleum." *Times Union,* 20 May 1997.
Deloria, Jr., Vine. "Laws Founded on Justice and Humanity: Reflections on the Content and Character of Federal Indian Law." *Arizona Law Review,* vol. 31 (fall 1989).
Deloria, Jr., Vine, and Clifford M. Lytle. *American Indians, American Justice.* Austin, TX: University of Texas Press, 1983.
Deloria, Jr., Vine, and Clifford M. Lytle. *The Nations Within: The Past and Future of American Indian Sovereignty.* New York: Pantheon Books, 1984.
Donovan, Bill. "Big Money Is Topic of Phoenix Meeting." *Navajo Times,* 9 January 1997.
"Early Inhabitants, Fur Trading, and Gold." http://www.factmonster.com/ce6/us/A0859754.html.
Egan, Dan. "Tribe Tests Treaty Laws on Hunting." *Idaho Falls Post Register,* 26 March 1995.
Esch, Mary. "Gambling Promoters Explore NY Casinos' Future at Gaming Summit." Associated Press State and Local Wire, 9 April 2002.
Evans, Matthew. "Sho-Ban to Charge Media to Report on Tribal Land." *Idaho Falls Post Register,* 4 January 2002.
Fadden, John. "Divisiveness at Akwesasne: Legacy of Nineteenth Century Colonialism." (1997) http://www.peacetree.com/akwesasne/division.htm.
Fadness, Gene and Lucille Edmo. "Tribe Refuses to Relinquish Hunting Rights." *Idaho Falls Post Register,* 20 December 1996.
Farsi, F. *Summary Information on the Shoshone-Bannock Tribes.* Land Use Department, Fort Hall, Idaho, March 1995.
Flick, Bob. "Idaho Senate Kills Bill that Promotes Tribal Slots." *Deseret News,* 27 March 2001.
Galston, William A. and Geoffrey L. Tibbetts. "Reinventing Federalism: The Clinton/Gore Program for a New Partnership among the Federal, State, Local, and Tribal Governments." *Publius: The Journal of Federalism* 24 (summer 1994).
Getches, David H. "Negotiated Sovereignty: Intergovernmental Agreements with

American Indian Tribes as Models for Expanding Self-Government." *Review of Constitutional Studies*, vol. 1, no. 1 (1993).
Getches, David H., Charles F. Wilkinson, and Robert A. Williams, Jr. *Federal Indian Law: Cases and Material*. 3d ed. St. Paul, MN: West Publishing Company, 1993.
Goldberg, Carole. *Public Law 280: State Jurisdiction over Reservation Indians*. Los Angeles: UCLA, American Indian Culture & Research Center, 1975.
Gover, B. K., C. B. Stetson, and S. M. Williams. *1994 Survey of Tribal Water Quality. The National Indian Policy*. Washington, D.C., September 1994.
Gover, B. K., C. B. Stetson, S. M. Williams, J. L. Walker, J. Marx, C. L. Hart, and C. Pearlman. "Tribal-State Dispute Resolution: Recent Attempts." *South Dakota Law Review* 36 (1991).
Hale, Albert and Louis Denetsosi. *The Navajo Nation: Title II Amendments of 1989*.
Hamilton, Candy. "Governor Janklow Meets with Oglala Tribal Leaders." *News from Indian Country*, August 1995.
Hamilton, Christopher and Donald T. Wells. *Federalism, Power, and Political Economy*. Englewood Cliffs, NJ: Prentice Hall, 1990.
Hannula, Dan. "Did State Double-Cross Puyallup Tribe?" *Seattle Times*, 27 November 1991.
Harris, LaDonna, Stephen Sachs, and Barbara Morris. "Honoring the Circle: Developing Government-to-Government Relations between Tribal Governments and the Federal, State, and Local Governments." Paper presented at the annual meeting of the Western Social Science Association, Albuquerque, NM, 2002.
"Historic Fort Hall." http://www.sho-ban.com/history.htm.
Indian Reorganization Act, 25 U.S.C.A., 461–478.
"Interstate Is Tied Up in Protest of Tax Deal." *New York Times*, 12 May 1997.
Jansen, Bart. "Tribes Turn to Former Military Bases." AP Online, 20 January 2000.
Johnson, Susan, Jeanne Kaufmann, John Dossett, and Sarah Hicks. *Government to Government: Understanding State and Tribal Governments*. Washington, D.C.: National Conference of State Legislatures, 2000.
"Judge Tosses Suit Over Tribal Resort Collecting Lodging Tax." Associated Press State and Local Wire, 28 February 2001.
Linthicum, Leslie. "Tribes Consider Roadblocks." *Albuquerque Journal*, 29 January 1998.
Loomis, Brandon. "Indian Hunting Rights to Be Subject of Trials." *Idaho Falls Post Register*, 31 December 1996.
Manning, Josh. "Sho-Ban Tribes, Astaris Reach Agreement on Wastewater Facility." *Idaho Falls Post Register*, 23 February 2001.
Mason, W. Dale. "Tribes and States: A New Era in Intergovernmental Affairs." *Publius: The Journal of Federalism* 28, no. 1 (1998).
McLeod, Lewis A. "The Development of the Confederated Salish and Kootenai Tribes of the Flathead Nation Tribal Air Quality Program." *Salish-Kootenai Tribal EPA*, September 1994.
McCool, Daniel. "Intergovernmental Conflict and Indian Water Rights: An Assessment of Negotiated Settlements." *Publius: The Journal of Federalism* 23 (winter 1993).
"Mohawk Leaders Deny Accord in Tax Dispute." *New York Times*, 21 May 1997.

Navajo Nation, Navajo Tribal Code, title 2, sec. 871, 1982.
"Navajos Worry Redistricting Will Water Down Their Clout." Associated Press State and Local Wire, 2 July 2001.
Nesbitt, Jim. "New Battles Ahead Over American Indian Sovereignty." *Las Vegas-Journal Review-Journal*, 3 October 1999.
Nice, David and Patricia Frederickson. *The Politics of Intergovernmental Relations*. Chicago: Nelson-Hall Publishers, 1995.
O'Brien, Sharon. *American Indian Tribal Governments*. Norman, OK: University of Oklahoma Press, 1989.
Odato, James. "Pataki Land Claim Tied to Casino." *Times Union*, 28 February 2002.
Odato, James. "Tribe, State Discuss Settling Land Claim: Eyeing Casino Deal, Mohawks Upbeat about Resolving Lawsuit." *Times Union*, 25 August 2001.
Office of the White House. "Government to Government Relations with Native American Tribal Governments," 29 April 1994.
"Pablo: Supreme Court Decision Reinforces Indian Fishing Rights in Montana." Associated Press State and Local Wire, 29 March 1999.
Philp, Kenneth. *John Collier's Crusade for Indian Reform*. Tucson, AZ: University of Arizona Press, 1978.
Pommersheim, Frank. "Tribal State Relations: Hope for the Future?" *South Dakota Law Review* 36 (1991).
Powell, Ronald. "U.S. Halts Shift of NTC Land to City: Ancestral-home Suit by Tribes to Be Heard First." *San Diego Union-Tribune*, 12 May 2000.
President William Clinton. Speech, 29 April 1994, http://www.his.gov/PublicInfo/publicAffairs/pressreleases/pressrelease1994/presmes.asp.
Price, Monroe. *Law and the American Indian: Readings, Notes, and Cases*. Indianapolis, IN: Bobbs-Merrill Co., 1973.
Prucha, Francis Paul. *The Great Father: The United States Government and the American Indians*. Lincoln, NE: University of Nebraska Press, 1984.
Public Law 280. 83-280, 67 Stat. 588.
"Puyallup Tribe Will Award Grants to Cities and County." *Seattle Post-Intelligencer*, 17 September 1998.
Reed, James B. and Judy A. Zelio. *States and Tribes: Building New Traditions*. Washington, D.C.: National Conference of State Legislatures, 1995.
Rolo, Mark Anthony. "Indians Will Resist Gorton's Attempts to Rewrite Laws." *Seattle Times*, 4 September 1997.
Ryser, Rudolph C. "When Tribes and States Collide: A Special Report Prepared for the Inter-Tribal Study Group on Tribal/State Relations 1995." http://www.cwis.org/FWDP/Americas/collide1.htm (2 October 1996).
"Salish-Kootenai Propose Closing Tribal Recreation Areas to Non-Members." Associated Press State and Local Wire, 20 April 1999.
Seely, Hart. "Landfill Near Massena Polluting Water Where Mohawk Children Played." *Syracuse Herald American*, 24 June 2001.
"Shoshone-Bannocks Could Cite Local Police on Reservation Land." Associated Press State and Local Wire, 25 October 2001.
Sly, Peter. "Federalism and Self-Determination: State Goals in Indian Rights Disputes." *Land and Water Law Review*, vol. 27, no. 1 (1992).
"Sovereignty Issue Cuts Lake County Bed Tax." Associated Press State and Local Wire, 24 March 1999.

"State Sues Over Tribal Resort's Refusal to Impose Bed Tax." Associated Press State and Local Wire, 9 October 2000.
Taule, Corey. "Protestors of 'Squaw' Get No Answers from Kempthorne." *Idaho Falls Post Register,* 10 March 2001.
Thomas, Katie. "Toxic Threats to Tribal Lands." *Albany Bureau,* 25 March 2001.
"Tribal Police Department Stripped of Authority after Road Block." Associated Press State and Local Wire, 3 March 2000.
U.S. Department of Commerce. *American Indian Reservation and Indian Trust Areas.* Washington, D.C.: U.S. Government Printing Office, 1996.
U.S. Environmental Protection Agency. *EPA Policy for the Administration of Environmental Programs on Indian Reservations.* 8 November 1984.
U.S. Environmental Protection Agency, Region 9. "Campo Band of Kumeyaay Indians' Environmental Success Story." *Indian Program News,* October 1998.
U.S. Environmental Protection Agency. "Source Specific Federal Implementation Plan for Navajo Generating Station." *Federal Register,* vol. 64, no. 173, 8 September 1999.
"Utah County to Add Indians to Jury Rolls." *Albuquerque Journal,* 30 June 1996.
Washington Governor's Office of Indian Affairs. http://www.goia.wa.gov/tribalinfo/puyallup.html.
Washington Review Code, 37.12.010 1976.
Wilkins, David E. *American Indian Politics and the American Political System.* New York: Rowman and Littlefield, 2002.
Wilkins, David E. "Reconsidering the Tribal-State Compact Process." *Policy Studies Journal,* vol. 22, no. 3 (1994).
Wilkinson, Charles F. and Eric R. Biggs. "The Evolution of the Termination Policy." *American Indian Law Review* 5 (1977).
Williams, Robert A., Jr., *The American Indian in Western Legal Thought: The Discourses of Conquest.* New York: Oxford University Press, 1990.
Wilson, James Q. *Bureaucracy.* New York: Basic Books, 1989.
Worsnop, Richard L. "Native Americans." *CQ Researcher,* vol. 2 (8 May 1992): 397.
Wright, Deil S. *Understanding Intergovernmental Relations.* Pacific Grove, CA: Brooks/Cole Publishing Company, 1988.
www.arizona.com/indians/navajo.html.
www.campo-kumeyaay.org/history.htm.
www.lewisandclark.state.mt.us/salish.htm.
www.nps.gov/ciro/cultural.htm.
www.nps.gov/nava/nav.htm.

Cases Cited

Canadian St. Regis Band of Mohawk Indians v. New York, 2nd District Court (2001).
Cherokee Nation v. Georgia, 30 U.S. (5 Pet.) 1, 8 L.Ed. 25 (1831).
Colorado River Conservation District v. United States, 424 U.S. at 820 (1976).
Donahue v. Justice Court, 15 CA, App. 3d, 557 (1971).
Idaho et al. v. Coeur d'Alene Tribe of Idaho et al., 94 U.S. 1474 (1997).
Johnson v. McIntosh, 21 U.S. (8 Wheat.) 543, 5L Ed 681 (1823).
Lone Wolf v. Hitchcock, 187 U.S. 553, 23 S.Ct. 216, 47 L. Ed. 299 (1903).

McClanahan v. Arizona State Tax Commission, 411 U.S. 164, 93 S.Ct. 1257, 36 L.Ed. 2d 129 (1973).
Native American Church v. Navajo Tribal Council, 272 F2d 131 (1959).
Navajo Nation v. United States, AZ, U.S. Court of Appeals Ninth Circuit (1982).
Organized Village of Kake v. Egan, 369 U.S. 60 (1962).
People v. Frank, 101 CA, App. 3d, Supp 8 (1979).
Puyallup Tribe v. Washington Gaming Department, 433 U.S. 165 (1977).
San Carlos Apache Tribe v. Arizona, 463 U.S. 545, 103 S.Ct. 3201, 77 L.ed. 2d. 837 (1983).
Seminole Tribe v. Florida, 517 U.S. 44 (1996).
United States v. Kagama, 118 U.S. 375, S.Ct. 1109, 30 L.Ed. 228 (1886).
United States v. McBratney, 104 U.S. 621 (1881).
Warren Trading Post v. Arizona Tax Commission, 380 U.S. 685 (1965).
Washington Department of Ecology v. Environmental Protection Agency, 752 F.2d 1465 9th Cir. (1985).
White Mountain Apache Tribe v. Bracker, 448 U.S. 136 (1980).
Williams v. Lee, 358 U.S. 217 (1959).
Worcester v. Georgia, 31 U.S. (6 Pet.) 515, 8 L.Ed. 483 (1832).

Interviews

Antonio, Patrick. April, 2002.
Ashley, Randy. June 2002.
Benedict, Les. February 1995 and 31 May 2002.
Bradley, Francis. April 2002.
Bryant, A. December 1995.
Clairmont, Les. June 2002.
Connolly, Mike. January 1995 and July 2002.
Farsi, F. March 1995.
Jock, K. February, 1995.
Kelly, D. May, 1995.
LaDucer, Rory. July 2002.
Martin, Mark. February 1995.
Martin, Shawn. July 2002.
Mcload, Lewis A. 1995.
Member of St. Regis Mohawk Tribal Police. 7 June 2002.
O'Connell, M. Seattle, Wash. July 1995.
Officials from the St. Regis Mohawk Tribe, Campo Band of Mission Indians, Navajo Nation, Shoshone-Bannock Tribe, Puyallup Tribe, and the Confederated Nation of the Salish and Kootenai. May 2002–August 2002.
Pablo, Gilbert. July 2002.
Sullivan, William. July 2002.
Teton, Elise. May 2002.
Thomas, Andrew. June 2002.
Trahant, Torrey. June 2002.
Tribal air official. August 2002.
Tribal water quality representative. June 2002.
Turner, Roger. March 1995 and June 2002.
Wolfley, Janet. May 2002.

Index

Air quality management, 47–49, 59–61, 71–72, 81–83, 94–96, 105–7
American Indian Policy Review Commission, 23
Arizona, 35, 39, 125; ADEQ policy for dealing with Indian tribes, 60; Arizona Department of Environmental Quality (ADEQ), 60–62; environmental management relations, 59–63; law enforcement relations, 63–64
Assimilation, 3, 18, 21–22, 29–30

Benedict, Les, 107
Bradley, Francis, 59
Bureau of Indian Affairs, 5, 7–8, 22, 52, 59
Bureau of Land Management, role in assisting tribal-state relations, 82

California: Act for the Government and Protection of Indians, 45; Act for the Relief of the Mission Indians in the State of California, 46; Assembly Bill-240, 47; California Environmental Quality Act, 49; environmental management relations, 47–50; law enforcement relations, 50–51
California Air Quality Control Board, 48
Campo Band of Kumeyaay Indians: air quality management relations, 47–49; governmental structure of, 47; law enforcement relations, 50–51; and reservation, 45–46; water quality management relations, 49–50
Campo Environmental Protection Agency, 47, 52–53
Canadian St. Regis Band of Mohawk Indians v. State of New York, 38
Carson, Kit, 58
Carter, Jimmy, and federal-tribal relations, 7
Catholic Church, 16
Champagne, Duane, 58
Checkerboard land pattern, 28, 30, 80–81, 84, 92, 61, 64, 119–20
Cherokee Nation v. Georgia, 19
Clean Air Act, 6
Clinton, William: and self-government, 24; and tribal-state-federal partnerships, 5–7, 24

Cohen, Felix, 16–17
Collier, John, 22
Colorado River Conservation District v. United States, 31. *See also* McCarren Amendment
Commission on Tribal-State Relations, 121–22
Connolly, Mike, 49–50, 54

Dawes Act. *See* General Allotment Act
Deloria, Vine, 4, 18
Devolution, 6–8
Dillon's Rule, 14
Doctrine of Discovery, 16
Donahue v. Justice Court, 37

Environmental Protection Agency (EPA), 8, 40, 48, 54, 59–60, 71–73, 82–84, 94–96, 106–8

Federalism, 3–5
Federal Trust Obligation, 18–21, 24–25, 28

Gaming: as source of conflict, 51–52, 100, 111–12; as potential for forging positive relations, 33, 75–76
General Allotment Act (Dawes Act), 21, 28, explained, 29–30; and checkerboarding, 30, 80–81, 84, 92

Hale, Albert, 65
Hunting and Fishing Rights, 37–38, 87–88, 99

Idaho: environmental management relations, 94–97; law enforcement relations, 97–98; perceived anti-Indian climate of, 97–99
Idaho et al. v. Coeur d'Alene Tribe of Idaho et al., 38
Indian Financing Act, 23
Indian Gaming Regulatory Act, 28; explained, 33–34
"The Indian Problem," 3, 22, 32
Indian Religious Freedom Act, 23

Indian Reorganization Act (IRA), 22, 39, 59, 93
Indian self-determination, 3, 5–6, 21, 23, 25
Indian Self-Determination and Education Assistance Act, 23
Indian Termination policy, 22, 32
Indian Tribal Economic Development and Contract Encouragement Act, 24

Johnson, Lyndon, federal-tribal relations, 7
Johnson v. McIntosh, 18

Land jurisdiction and land claims issues, 38–39, 54, 111–12
Law enforcement, 50–51, 63–64, 74–75, 84–86, 97–98, 109–10
Lewis and Clark Expedition: and the Salish, 79–80; and the Shoshone, 91–92
Litigation, as an obstacle to tribal state cooperation, 36–39, 83
Lone Wolf v. Hitchcock, 21, 29
Long Walk, 58

Marshall, John, 18–19
Marshall Trilogy, 18–20, 25, 29. See also *Johnson v. McIntosh; Cherokee Nation v. Georgia;* and *Worcester v. Virginia*
Mashantucket Pequot Tribe, 33
Mason, W. Dale, 36
McCarren Amendment, 30–31
McClanahan v. Arizona State Tax Commission, 14, 35
Mille Lacs Band of Chippewa, 88
Montana: air quality relations, 81–82; law enforcement relations, 84–86; location of Flathead Reservation, 80; water quality relations, 83–84

National Council on Indian Opportunity, 23
National Indian Policy Center, 123
Native American Church v. Navajo Tribal Council, 27, 36–37

Navajo Nation, 35, 39, 122 ; air quality management relations, 59–61; civil rights concerns of, 65–66; and establishment of reservation, 58; governmental structure of, 59; law enforcement relations, 63–64; and "lesson in sovereign rights," 65; and Navajo Environmental Protection Agency, 60–62; and 1992 statement of policy on entering into agreements with New Mexico, 61; opposition to IRA, 59; water quality management relations, 61–63

Navajo Nation v. U.S., State of Arizona, 39

New Mexico: and environmental relations with Navajo Nation, 61–63; and law enforcement relations, 63

New York: environmental management relations, 106–9; law enforcement relations, 109–10; Operation Gallant Piper, 111

Nixon, Richard: and "New Federalism," 5–8; and self determination, 5, 23

Organized Village of Kake v. Egan, 35

Pelkey, Jack, 109–10
People v. Frank, 37
Plenary power of Congress, 20–22, 27
Pommersheim, Frank, 4, 17
Public Law 280, 28, 31–34, 38–39; and law enforcement issues, 50, 84–85, 97–98; and retro cession of authority, 84–85
Puget Sound Air Pollution Control Agency, 72
Puget Sound Energy Corporation, 73
Puyallup Land Claims Settlement Agreement, 70–71
Puyallup Tribe, 37; air quality management relations, 71–72; and creation of reservation, 69; governmental structure of, 71; law enforcement relations, 74–75;
Puyallup Department of the Environment, 72–73; water quality management relations, 72–74
Puyallup Tribe v. Washington Gaming Department, 37

Roosevelt, Theodore, and attitude toward the Dawes Act, 29

Safe Drinking Water Act, 6
St. Regis Mohawk Nation: air quality management relations, 105–7; governmental structure of, 104–5; law enforcement relations, 109–10; and Mohawk Council, 104; and Mohawk National Council, 104; and St. Regis Mohawk Tribal Council, 104; and the Warrior Society, 105
Salish-Kootenai Tribes: air quality relations, 81–83; and creation of reservation, 80; governmental structure of, 80–81; law enforcement, 84–86; water quality relations, 83–84
San Carlos Apache Tribe v. Arizona, 31. See also McCarren Amendment
San Diego County: and contributions to Campo air problems, 48; and perceived limit on tribal economic development, 49–55
Seminole Tribe v. Florida, 33, See also Indian Gaming Regulatory Act
Shoshone-Bannock Tribes: air quality management relations, 94–96; and the "Day of the Run," 92; and Fort Hall Land Use Department, 93; governmental structure of, 93; law enforcement relations, 97–98; and reservation, 92–93; water quality management relations, 96–97
Smoke shops, as source of tension, 75
Sovereignty and self-government, 3–5, 14, 18–22, 24, 27–28, 31–32, 34–37, 49, 111, 123
Supremacy clause, 14

Taxation issues, 75, 86–87, 110–11
Thompson, Tommy, 34

Treaties, 16–18, 25, 27–28, 46, 57–58; Treaty of Fort Bridger, 92, 99; Treaty of Hell Gate, 80, 88; Treaty of Medicine Creek, 69; Treaty of Soda Springs, 92

Tribal land ownership and right to occupy; 18. *See also* Checkerboard land pattern

Tribal Self-government Act, 24

Tribes as states, 7–8, 36–37

Turner, Roger, 95–96

Turtle Cove, pollution in, 107–8

United States Supreme Court, and shaping of Indian Policy, 4–5, 18. *See also individual case listings*

United States v. McBratney, 34

US v. Kagama, 20, 29, 34

Victoria, Francisco De, 16–18

Warren Trading Post v. Arizona Tax Commission, 35

Washington (state): Department of Ecology, 73–74; environmental management relations, 71–74; Gaming Department, 37; law enforcement relations, 74–75

Water quality management, 49–50, 61–63, 72–74, 83–84, 96–97, 107–9

Water rights disputes, 31, 39, 83–84, 96–97

White Mountain Apache Tribe v. Bracker, 36

Wilkins, David, 4, 24, 122

Williams, Terry, 40

Williams v. Lee, 35; and the infringement test, 35–36

Winters Doctrine, 30–31

Worcester v. Georgia, 19, 27, 34–35, 45

About the Author

JEFFREY S. ASHLEY is Assistant Professor of Political Science, Eastern Illinois University. In addition to essays in published collections, he is the co-author, with Zachary Smith, of *Groundwater Politics and Policy in the West*.

SECODY J. HUBBARD is Tribal Air Quality Liaison for the United States Environmental Protection Agency (USEPA).